Seaboard To Sideboard

Seaboard To Sideboard

A collection of recipes from the Junior League of Wilmington, North Carolina

This cookbook is a collection of favorite recipes, which are not necessarily original recipes. Published by the Junior League of Wilmington, North Carolina, Inc.

Seaboard to Sideboard
Copyright© 1998 by
Junior League of Wilmington, North Carolina, Inc.
3803 Wrightsville Avenue
Downey Branch Office Park, Unit 9
Wilmington, North Carolina 28403
910-799-7405

Photography by Melinda Strawn Vass

Historical Vignettes of Wilmington, N.C. and the Lower Cape Fear
©1997 by Glenda Hallman Bradley and Angie Chatham Cline

Library of Congress Catalog Number: 98-070143
ISBN: 0-9607822-0-6

Edited, Designed, and Manufactured by Favorite Recipes® Press
an imprint of

FRP™

P.O. Box 305142, Nashville, Tennessee 37230
800-358-0560

Art Director: Steve Newman
Designer: David Malone and Pam Cole
Book Project Manager: Linda A. Jones

Manufactured in the United States of America
First Printing: 1998 15,000 copies

PUBLICATIONS COMMITTEE

Chairman: Mary Jefferies, Ad Hoc (1996–97), Ann McCall-Moore (1996–97), Kim Whitfield (1996–97)

Chairman: Angie Chatham Cline (1997–99)

Treasurer: Mary High (1997–99)

Special Events Coordinator: Krista Combs Ray (1997–99)

Art and Design: Mary Jefferies, Katherine Marapese, Krista Combs Ray, Becky Shannon Spivey

Recipe Collection: Glenda H. Bradley, Angie Chatham Cline, Barbara McInnes

Inter League Marketing: Margaret Lamm, Mary Beth Laurie, René Lank Sasser, Angela Babb Turner

Policies and Procedures: Angie Chatham Cline, Mary High, Ann McCall-Moore

Preface: Angela Babb Turner

Fund-Raising: Angie Chatham Cline, Ann McCall-Moore, Kim Whitfield

Chef's Section: Margaret Lamm, Mary Beth Laurie, Angela Babb Turner

Menu Section: Angie Chatham Cline, Barbara McInnes, Ann McCall-Moore, Angela Babb Turner

Advisory Committee: Estelle Baker, Angie Chatham Cline, Becky Edwards, Mary High,
Ann McCall-Moore, Suzanne Nash, Krista Combs Ray, Margaret Robison

Testing: Angie Chatham Cline, Ann McCall-Moore

Historical Vignettes written by: Glenda H. Bradley, Angie Chatham Cline

Publications Committee: Glenda H. Bradley, Catherine Nixon Cheek, Angie Chatham Cline,
Cathy Cypher, Catherine Barrett-Fischer, Mary High, Mary Jefferies, Robyn Brickner Krassas,
Margaret Lamm, Mary Beth Laurie, Katherine Marapese, Barbara McInnes, Ann McCall-Moore,
Sallie Lynch Price, Krista Combs Ray, René Lank Sasser, Becky Shannon Spivey,
Cackie Stephenson, Angela Babb Turner, Kim Whitfield

STATEMENT OF PURPOSE

The Junior League of Wilmington, North Carolina, Inc.,
is an organization of women committed to promoting voluntarism,
to developing the potential of women, and to improving the community
through the effective action and leadership of trained volunteers.
Its purpose is exclusively educational and charitable.
The Junior League of Wilmington reaches out to women
of all races, religions, and national origins who demonstrate
an interest in the commitment to voluntarism.

VISION STATEMENT

The Junior League of Wilmington, Inc. (JLW), will be a community leader
in creating positive change in the lives of children and families.

Denotes recipe previously published in *Seafood Sorcery*.

Denotes recipe previously published in *Nothing Could Be Finer*.

Denotes recipe previously published in *Best of the Best from North Carolina*.

Bake your preschooler's favorite muffins and watch his eyes light up. Surprise your wife with breakfast
in bed and brighten her early morning face into a smile. Prepare a picnic dinner for your husband and enjoy the
laughter as you both relax. These simple moments are gently etched into memory and they, too,
become *history*. Long after the dishes are washed and put away, this history lingers,
helping to create and sustain happy, healthy families.

In 1923, the Junior League of Wilmington launched a campaign to promote the health and well-being of
Wilmington's families. That year, local social workers requested assistance and nineteen women responded by
forming the Charity League. More than seven decades and two name changes later, the Junior League of
Wilmington, Inc., now dedicates itself to "creating positive change in the lives of families" through the
volunteer activities of more than five hundred active and sustaining members.

Since the early 1920s, the Junior League has initiated and assisted many family health programs.
Most of these programs have aspired to improve the health of area children. From staffing Well Baby clinics to
screening for vision impairment in the Prevent Blindness Project, the Junior League has worked to
secure a healthier tomorrow for local children. Along the way, the League has developed and assisted many
programs, including the Children's Festival, an event highlighting support agencies for children,
and Sunrise Kids, a children's grief counseling program.

The Junior League of Wilmington has supported the development of healthy minds and bodies
through educational, cultural, and recreational programs. All New Hanover County fifth graders participate in Sea
Scholars, a marine science curriculum developed in collaboration with the North Carolina Aquarium at Fort Fisher.
Each year, Pied Piper Theater, in conjunction with Thalian Hall Center of the Performing Arts, Inc., and the
New Hanover County Board of Education, presents an orchestrated production for more than seven thousand
school children in the first and second grades. Hundreds of girls meet for after-school activities at
Girls Incorporated of Wilmington, a club the League helped establish in 1935.

The community at large has also benefited from many Junior League programs. Since its inception,
the League has championed arts, historic preservation, and education. Sponsoring North Carolina Symphony
concerts, co-sponsoring historic tours with the Lower Cape Fear Historical Society, and financing a pilot

plan for the restoration of Thalian Hall represent just a few of the League's efforts at illuminating Wilmington's cultural and historical atmosphere. Further efforts include the publication of the *Guide Book to Wilmington*, the *Old Wilmington Guidebook*, and *Wilmington North Carolina: An Architectural and Historical Portrait*. Friends of the Library and the League's Library Task Force successfully served as advocates for the relocation and expansion of the New Hanover County Public Library. Additionally, the League played a large role in developing the Michael Jordan Discovery Gallery for the Cape Fear Museum.

Over the years, the League has contributed financial assistance to many organizations. Project Graduation, Hospital Hospitality House, the Domestic Violence Shelter, and the Child Advocacy Commission benefit the welfare of children and families. The Wilmington Arts Council, WHQR Public Radio, and Thalian Hall Center for the Performing Arts add to Wilmington's rich artistic diversity. Meals on Wheels and the Hospice Festival of Trees provide valuable services to the community.

Junior League of Wilmington fund-raisers have made all the programs and contributions possible. From collard sales to bargain sales, golf tournaments to the Holiday Shopping Gala, as Wilmington has grown, so have the fund-raising efforts of the League. Two cookbooks, *Seafood Sorcery* and *Nothing Could Be Finer*, preceded *Seaboard to Sideboard*. The pages of these cookbooks have provided financial foundations for many worthy programs and delicious recipes for many fine southern meals.

The nineteenth-century English theologian A. P. Stanley* once observed, "Each of us is bound to make the little circle in which he lives better and happier. Bound to see that out of that small circle the widest good may flow." The history of your home is punctuated with the smiles, concern, and heritage which often surround the dining table. Likewise, the history of our community is augmented by the hope, care, and tradition that surround our city. Your purchase of *Seaboard to Sideboard* will contribute to both. Thank you for supporting the Junior League of Wilmington, Inc.

All League information is from the *Junior League of Wilmington, Inc., Handbook*.

*Bradley, G. Granville, "Stanley, Arthur Penrhyn." *The Encyclopaedia Britannica*. 9th edition, 1894.

ACKNOWLEDGMENTS

We would like to thank the following people for contributing their time and
invaluable support to make this book possible.

Estelle Baker	The Fisherman's Wife	Murrow Furniture Galleries
Ede D. Baldridge	Louise Gorham	Suzanne Nash
James Rush Beeler, Ph.D.	Dorothy Guggenheimer	Margaret Robison
Blockade Runner Resort Hotel	Carl K. Henry	Anne Russell, Ph.D.
and Conference Center	Beth Howard	Bill Reaves
Mr. and Mrs. Al Butler	Barbara Bear Jamison	Carolyn B. Thomason
Bill Cline	Bobbie Jefferies	Melinda Strawn Vass
Nancy Crnich	The Lilly Pad	Claudia Vurnakes
Becky Edwards		Gibbs Willard

A special thank you to the North Carolina Azalea Festival Committee for making
Seaboard to Sideboard the official cookbook of the North Carolina Azalea Festival.

ABOUT THE PHOTOGRAPHER

Melinda Strawn Vass has lived in Wilmington all of her life. Being a native gives
her a unique perspective when photographing the coastal area and historic sites. Melinda
also photographs family portraits and business brochures. Her career includes
professional photography and a family-owned and -operated business. In her leisure,
Melinda enjoys boating and fishing with her husband Jimmy and their son.

PHOTOGRAPHY FOOD STYLIST

Krista Combs Ray

INTRODUCTION

"Throughout my life, as I have lived in many cities in many different states,
I have returned to Wilmington, North Carolina, for sustenance, for Wilmington
to me is home. It is a very special place where the air is soft with salt moisture,
the trees are hung with gray moss and ornamented with creamy magnolia,
the fiery azalea and variegated hydrangea bloom, the sun rises over the ocean
and sets beyond the river, the sandy earth is strewn with huge pine cones
and sprightly gaillardia, the falls are golden, the winters are mild,
the springs are sweet, and the summers are filled with frolic.
Wilmington is oyster roasts, swimming, sailing, bare feet, and long slow walks
down plaza-lined streets. In Wilmington I can hear the voices of my ancestors
whispering in high-ceilinged rooms and on windswept sounds and beaches.
The Wilmington panorama stimulates a sense of heritage in those born
within its boundaries and a sense of excitement in newcomers and visitors,
making us wish to remain a lifetime here, or at the least,
to come to visit again and again."

—*Anne Russell*

Excerpt from *Wilmington: A Pictorial History,* by Anne Russell, Ph.D.

Appetizers

WELCOME!

Seaboard to Sideboard—

enjoy a generous serving of Southern hospitality. We invite you to capture the full essence of the Lower Cape Fear Region. Journey through humble beginnings to a time of lavish living when the common thread was hospitality. Sample our foods, learn a little about our history, our heritage, and our colorful and legendary people. Our early settlers molded our regional character, their festive ways often seen in the traditions we have kept and adapted for our own. The best of the past remains in the people and the hospitality they share. Experience our timeless tastes and traditions. Be our guest and savor the Cape Fear.

RED PEPPER AND CHUTNEY CHEESE SPREAD

1	large red bell pepper, chopped
1	medium red onion, chopped
3/4	teaspoon curry powder
1	tablespoon olive oil
1/3	cup mango chutney
2	tablespoons dry sherry
1/4	teaspoon salt
4	to 6 drops of liquid red pepper seasoning
1	cup farmer cheese or light cream cheese

Add the red bell pepper, onion and curry powder to the heated olive oil in a skillet. Cook over medium heat for 10 to 12 minutes or until the vegetables are soft, stirring occasionally. Stir in the chutney and sherry. Cook for 1 minute and remove from heat. Sprinkle with the salt and red pepper seasoning. Add the cheese and mix well. Spoon into a serving dish. Let stand until cool. Chill, tightly wrapped with plastic wrap, for 4 hours or longer. Serve with assorted crackers, as a dip for fresh vegetables or as a sandwich spread. May prepare up to 2 days in advance and store in the refrigerator. Yield: 2 cups.

Note: May prepare in the microwave by combining the red pepper, onion, curry powder and olive oil in a round shallow 9-inch glass dish. Microwave on High for 8 minutes, stirring twice. Stir in the chutney and sherry. Microwave on High for 2 minutes. Continue as in the conventional method above.

Hummus with Red Pepper and Pimentos

2	(15-ounce) cans garbanzos
2	cloves of garlic, crushed
1/3	cup tahini
1	tablespoon crushed red pepper
2	tablespoons lemon juice
2	tablespoons olive oil
1	(4-ounce) jar pimentos, drained

Combine the garbanzos, garlic, tahini, red pepper, lemon juice and olive oil in a blender container. Process until the mixture is smooth. Fold in the pimentos. Spoon into a serving bowl. Serve with toasted pita wedges. May also use as a sandwich spread. Yield: 12 servings.

Vidalia Onion Dip

2	cups chopped Vidalia onions
2	cups finely shredded Swiss cheese
2	cups mayonnaise
2	tablespoons grated Parmesan cheese

Combine the Vidalia onions, Swiss cheese and mayonnaise in a bowl and mix well. Spoon into a lightly greased 1-quart baking dish. Sprinkle with the Parmesan cheese. Bake at 325 degrees for 40 to 45 minutes or until bubbly. Yield: 12 to 15 servings.

CLAUDE HOWELL'S CRAB MOUSSE

Tribute to Claude Howell (1915-1997)

The Junior League of Wilmington, North Carolina, is fortunate to have had the support of Claude Howell. The recipient of numerous accolades for his artistic career, he shared his creativity and talent with his community. A fifty-year association between Dr. Howell and the Junior League of Wilmington began in the 1930s when he was a chorus boy in the follies. In the 1970s, through the University of North Carolina at Wilmington, he taught an art history course for Junior League volunteers who then lectured in public schools. His artwork, depicting man and the sea, graced the cover of the 1990 edition of the Junior League of Wilmington cookbook *Seafood Sorcery*. His contributions to the city of Wilmington are a lasting legacy.

1	envelope unflavored gelatin
3	tablespoons hot water
1	cup whipping cream, whipped
1	pound fresh white crab meat, drained, flaked
1	onion, finely chopped
1/2	cup white wine
2	tablespoons drained capers
1 1/2	tablespoons lemon juice
1	teaspoon Worcestershire sauce
1	teaspoon hot Chinese mustard
1	teaspoon celery seeds
1/8	teaspoon Tabasco sauce
·	Chopped fresh dillweed or tarragon to taste
·	Lettuce leaves
·	Cherry tomatoes
·	Sliced olives
1	(4-ounce) jar pimentos, drained

Dissolve the unflavored gelatin in the hot water in a small bowl. Let stand until cool. Fold into the whipped cream in a large bowl. Chill for 15 to 30 minutes or until partially set. Combine the crab meat, onion, wine, capers, lemon juice, Worcestershire sauce, mustard, celery seeds, Tabasco sauce and dillweed in a bowl and mix well. Fold into the partially set gelatin mixture. Spoon into a greased fish mold. Chill for 8 to 10 hours or until set. Unmold onto a serving platter lined with lettuce leaves and dotted with cherry tomatoes. Decorate the fish mousse with olives for eyes and pimentos for fins and gills. Serve with melba toast. Yield: 8 to 10 servings.

Note: Use 2 envelopes unflavored gelatin and 6 tablespoons hot water on summer days when the weather is hot and humid.

Giovanni da Verrazano, the first European explorer to see the Carolina coast, arrived at the mouth of the Cape Fear River on July 8, 1524. The name "Cape Fear" speaks of the treacherous shoals and currents marking the mouth of the river and reaching far out into the sea. Settlers led by John Vassall of Barbados established Charles Town on the west bank of the Cape Fear River in 1664. In 1670 the Barbadians established a second Charles Town farther south, now known as Charleston, South Carolina.

▶

CLASSIC COASTAL CRAB MEAT SPREAD

8	ounces cream cheese, softened
1/2	cup mayonnaise
1	tablespoon minced onion
1	tablespoon cocktail sauce
1/4	teaspoon Worcestershire sauce
1	pound fresh lump crab meat, drained, flaked
·	Watercress
·	Assorted crackers or fresh vegetables

Combine the cream cheese, mayonnaise, onion, cocktail sauce and Worcestershire sauce in a food processor container. Process until the mixture is blended. Stir in the crab meat. Spoon into a serving bowl. Garnish with watercress. Serve with assorted crackers or fresh vegetables for dipping. Yield: 8 to 10 servings.

SUN-DRIED TOMATO AND GOAT CHEESE APPETIZER

8	ounces Montrachet cheese
1	(2-ounce) jar oil-pack sun-dried tomatoes
1/4	cup virgin olive oil
3	tablespoons chopped fresh basil leaves
·	Freshly cracked peppercorns to taste
1	loaf ciabatta or fresh French bread, thinly sliced
1	clove of garlic, crushed

Bring all ingredients to room temperature. Place the cheese on a serving platter. Arrange the tomatoes over the cheese. Drizzle with the olive oil. Sprinkle with the basil and pepper. Rub the bread slices with the garlic. Arrange the bread around the spread. Yield: 10 servings.

In 1725 a group led by Colonel Maurice Moore and his son Judge Maurice Moore settled Brunswick Town close to the original Charles Town site—sixteen miles south of present-day Wilmington.

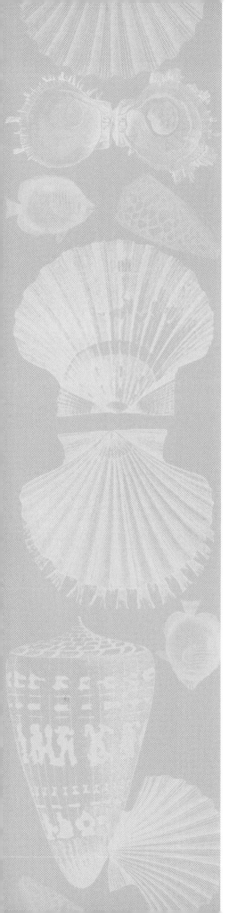

CRANBERRY JALAPEÑO SALSA

1	orange
2	cups fresh or thawed frozen cranberries
2/3	cup sugar
1/8	teaspoon salt
1/2	medium green bell pepper, chopped
1	to 2 jalapeños, seeded, finely chopped
3	tablespoons chopped fresh cilantro
1/4	cup chopped pecans

Cut the orange into quarters and remove the seeds. Process the unpeeled orange quarters in a food processor until coarsely chopped, scraping the side once. Add the cranberries, sugar and salt. Pulse 2 to 3 times or until the cranberries are coarsely chopped. Spoon into a bowl. Add the green pepper, jalapeños, cilantro and pecans and mix well. Spoon into a serving bowl. Chill, covered, for 2 hours or longer before serving. Serve with potato chips, sweet potato chips or turkey. Yield: 3 cups.

CREAMY MAPLE DIP FOR FRUIT

8	ounces cream cheese, softened
1/2	cup sour cream
1/4	cup sugar
1/4	cup packed brown sugar
1	to 2 tablespoons maple syrup

Beat the cream cheese in a mixer bowl until smooth. Add the sour cream, sugar, brown sugar and maple syrup and mix well. Chill, covered, in the refrigerator. Serve with sliced fresh fruit. Yield: 2 cups.

SPICY SHRIMP BALL

8	ounces cream cheese, softened
1	pound boiled shrimp, peeled, chopped
½	small onion, minced
⅛	teaspoon Worcestershire sauce
2	tablespoons mayonnaise
•	Juice of ½ lemon
¼	teaspoon garlic powder
¼	teaspoon salt
•	Chopped fresh parsley
•	Paprika

Mix the cream cheese in a bowl until smooth. Stir in the shrimp, onion, Worcestershire sauce, mayonnaise, lemon juice, garlic powder and salt. Shape into a ball. Sprinkle with parsley and paprika. Place on a serving plate. Serve with assorted crackers. Yield: 10 to 12 servings.

MARINATED SHRIMP

10	pounds shrimp
1	cup seafood seasoning
3½	cups vegetable oil
2	cups white vinegar
1	tablespoon salt
3	tablespoons plus 1 teaspoon celery seeds
6	cups sliced onions
½	cup plus 2 tablespoons capers
12	to 15 bay leaves

Boil the shrimp and seafood seasoning in water to cover in a large stockpot until the shrimp turn pink. Drain and peel the shrimp. Combine the vegetable oil, vinegar, salt, celery seeds, onions, capers and bay leaves in a large container and mix well. Add the peeled shrimp. Marinate, covered, in the refrigerator for 24 hours or longer. Drain and discard the bay leaves before serving. Yield: 25 servings.

BASIL AND FETA CHEESE TRIANGLES

1	pound feta cheese, crumbled
2	large eggs, lightly beaten
¼	cup finely chopped fresh basil
¼	teaspoon white pepper
1	(16-ounce) package frozen phyllo dough, thawed
¼	cup melted butter or margarine

Mash the feta cheese in a bowl with a fork. Add the eggs, basil and white pepper and mix well. Cut the stack of phyllo dough into 3 equal portions lengthwise. Arrange 2 strips of the phyllo dough in a stack, keeping the remaining phyllo dough covered with waxed paper and a damp cloth. Place 1 heaping teaspoonful of the cheese filling on the end of the stack. Fold in a triangular shape end over end to the opposite end to enclose the filling. Place on a baking sheet greased with shortening. Brush the triangle with butter. Repeat with the remaining phyllo dough and filling.

Bake at 350 degrees for 20 minutes or until puffed and golden brown. Serve warm. May chill the triangles, covered, for 24 hours before baking. May freeze the triangles, tightly covered, for up to 2 months and increase the baking time by 5 minutes. May use shredded Monterey Jack cheese instead of feta cheese and substitute 1 tablespoon dried basil for the fresh. Yield: 36 servings.

Early settlers of the Lower Cape Fear Region found swamps, cypress trees, alligators, and the world's most curious carnivore, the Venus flytrap. It is native in only one place in the world, a sixty-mile radius of Wilmington. In 1763 Governor Arthur Dobbs called the plant "the great wonder of the vegetable world." To Charles Darwin, it was "the most wonderful plant in the world." Sometime after World War II, Wilmington florist Will Rehder came upon a flytrap holding the body of a lifeless frog.

➤

GOUGÈRE

This appetizer makes a nice presentation and is good served
with red wine.

1	cup water
6	tablespoons butter
1	teaspoon salt
1/8	teaspoon pepper
1	cup flour
4	eggs
1	cup plus 2 tablespoons shredded Gruyère cheese

Bring the water, butter, salt and pepper to a boil in a saucepan. Add the
flour all at once, stirring constantly for 1 minute or until the mixture forms a ball.
Remove from the heat. Add the eggs 1 at a time, beating well after each addition.
Stir in 1 cup of the cheese. Drop the dough by tablespoonfuls with the sides touching
into an 8- or 9-inch circle on a lightly greased baking sheet. Sprinkle with the
remaining 2 tablespoons cheese. Bake at 425 degrees for 30 to 45 minutes or
until puffed and golden brown. Slice into wedges and serve immediately.
Yield: 6 to 8 servings.

His photograph of this unique specimen was featured in Life Magazine. Robert Ripley declared that it was the most unusual study of combined plant and animal life ever to come to his attention as editor of Believe It or Not.

An old legend says that in 1718 Stede Bonnet, the infamous "Gentleman Pirate," sailed up the Cape Fear River to replenish provisions at the plantation of a reformed crew member. When the old comrade left to attend to business elsewhere, the buccaneers kidnapped his beautiful young bride and set sail down the Cape Fear. As the pirate ship neared the lone cypress known to all as the Dram Tree, the brave wife slipped overboard unnoticed and swam into the sanctuary of the old tree's low-hanging moss-draped boughs. There she hid until morning when her husband rescued her from her arbor hiding place.

BAKED HERB HAVARTI CHEESE

Superb. Guests will gather around to sample this fabulous hors d'oeuvre.

2	tablespoons Dijon mustard
12	ounces Havarti cheese
1	tablespoon parsley flakes
1	tablespoon chopped fresh dillweed
1	teaspoon fennel seeds
1	teaspoon chopped fresh basil
1	sheet frozen puff pastry, thawed
1	egg, beaten

Spread the mustard over the cheese. Sprinkle with the parsley flakes, dillweed, fennel seeds and basil. Place the pastry over the top of the cheese and turn over. Wrap the cheese in the pastry to enclose as for a present, trimming excess pastry and brushing the seams with water to seal. Place seam side down on a plate. Chill, covered, in the refrigerator for 30 minutes or for up to 8 to 10 hours. Place on a greased baking sheet. Bake at 375 degrees for 20 minutes. Brush with the egg. Bake for 10 minutes. Remove from the oven and let stand for 5 minutes before serving. Serve with sliced pears and sliced Fuji or Golden Delicious apples. May also serve with assorted crackers. Yield: 12 to 15 servings.

CARAMELIZED ONION TARTLETS

2	large Spanish or Vidalia onions
1	tablespoon unsalted butter
1	tablespoon vegetable oil
1	tablespoon sugar
·	Sesame Seed Pastry
2	eggs
3/4	cup milk
1/8	teaspoon salt

Cut the onions into thin slices; cut the slices into halves. Heat the butter and oil in a large skillet over medium heat. Add the onions and sugar. Cook for 15 minutes or until the onions are caramelized medium to dark brown, stirring frequently; do not burn. Remove from the heat and let cool slightly. Roll the Sesame Seed Pastry 1/8 inch thick on a lightly floured surface. Cut into twenty-six 3-inch circles. Press the circles into greased 2 1/2- to 3-inch tartlet pans. Spoon the onion mixture into the pastry-lined pans. Beat the eggs, milk and salt in a small bowl. Pour over the onion mixture in the prepared pans. Bake at 400 degrees for 20 minutes or until set. Serve warm or chilled. May prepare the onion mixture 2 days ahead and chill, covered, in the refrigerator. Bring to room temperature before using.
Yield: 26 tartlets.

SESAME SEED PASTRY

1 1/3	cups flour
1/4	cup sesame seeds
1/4	teaspoon salt
1/2	cup unsalted butter, cut into small pieces
3	to 4 tablespoons cold water

Mix the flour, sesame seeds and salt in a medium bowl. Cut in the butter until crumbly. Add the cold water 1 tablespoon at a time, mixing with a fork until the mixture is just moist enough to hold together. Shape into a ball. Wrap in plastic wrap. Chill for 1 hour or for up to 3 days, bringing to room temperature before rolling the pastry dough. May freeze the dough for up to 6 weeks.

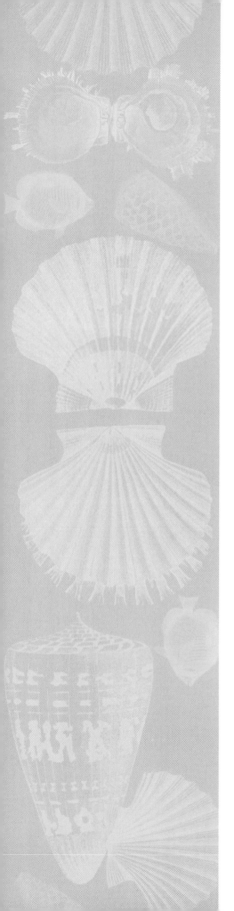

DIJON CHICKEN TIDBITS

4	whole chicken breasts, boned, skinned
1/4	cup butter
2	teaspoons Dijon mustard
1	clove of garlic, crushed
1	tablespoon minced parsley
1	teaspoon lemon juice
1/8	teaspoon salt
1/4	cup dry fine bread crumbs
1/4	cup grated Parmesan cheese

Cut the chicken into small bite-size pieces. Melt the butter in a 12-inch skillet over medium heat. Stir in the mustard, garlic, parsley, lemon juice and salt. Add the chicken. Sauté for 5 to 10 minutes or until light brown. Remove from the heat. Sprinkle with the bread crumbs and Parmesan cheese. Toss until the chicken is evenly coated. Place on a serving platter. Serve warm with small wooden or plastic picks. Yield: 75 pieces.

TEXAS FIRECRACKERS

2	(22-ounce) jars pepperoncini, drained
6	ounces Monterey Jack cheese with peppers
1	(6-ounce) boneless skinless chicken breast, cooked
24	sheets frozen phyllo dough, thawed
48	long fresh chives or green onion stems

Select twenty-four 2-inch-long pepperoncini, reserving the remaining pepperoncini for garnish. Remove the stems and seeds and discard. Drain the peppers thoroughly on paper towels. Cut the cheese into twenty-four 1/4x1 1/2-inch rectangles. Cut the chicken into 24 pieces. Stuff each of the drained peppers with 1 piece of cheese and 1 piece of chicken.

Arrange 4 sheets of the phyllo dough in a stack, spraying each sheet with butter-flavor nonstick cooking spray. Keep the remaining phyllo dough covered with a damp cloth to prevent drying out. Cut the stacked phyllo sheets into halves lengthwise and then cut crosswise. Place 1 stuffed pepper on the long end of each phyllo stack and roll up, twisting the ends to seal. Place on a baking sheet. Repeat with the remaining phyllo dough and stuffed peppers.

Bake at 375 degrees for 20 minutes or until golden brown. Tie the twisted ends of the pastry with chives. Place on a serving platter and garnish with the remaining pepperoncini. Serve immediately. May freeze the unbaked firecrackers in an airtight container for up to 3 months. Yield: 24 servings.

SEVICHE

Excellent to serve as a first course for dinner parties since it may be prepared ahead of time.

Excellent to serve as a first course for dinner parties since it may be prepared ahead of time.

1½	pounds fresh white fish fillets, such as red snapper, halibut, Atlantic cod, flounder or drum
½	cup lemon juice
½	cup lime juice
½	cup olive oil
2	cloves of garlic, crushed
½	teaspoon oregano
½	teaspoon thyme
1	teaspoon ground coriander or cilantro
·	Tabasco sauce to taste
·	Freshly ground pepper to taste
1	green or red bell pepper, finely chopped
4	green onions, chopped
2	tomatoes, chopped
1	tablespoon minced fresh mint

Cut the fish into small thin slices. Place in a bowl with a mixture of the lemon juice and lime juice. Marinate, covered, in the refrigerator for 2 hours. Combine the olive oil, garlic, oregano, thyme, coriander, Tabasco sauce and pepper in a bowl and mix well. Stir in the bell pepper, green onions, tomatoes and mint. Add the marinated fish and stir gently. Chill, covered, in the refrigerator for 1 hour. May also use fresh water bass or bream in this recipe. Yield: 6 to 8 servings.

Note: The acid in the lemon and lime juices "cooks" and turns the fish opaque. Use only fresh fish in this recipe.

In 1667 settlers abandoned the Charles Town settlement on the Cape Fear River and the pirates moved in. Present-day Southport became a sanctuary for buccaneers who were conducting raiding parties on the ships trading with Charleston. Colonel William Rhett of South Carolina led an expedition to Cape Fear to put an end to the piracy. On September 27, 1718, a fierce battle raged in the Cape Fear River between Rhett's two vessels, Sea Nymph and Henry, and Stede Bonnet's Royal James.

▶

SHRIMP PUFFS

1	quart shrimp
1	bay leaf
·	Old Bay seasoning to taste
1	large onion grated
2	teaspoons salt
16	ounces cream cheese, softened
1/2	cup mayonnaise
1/4	cup catsup
1/4	cup prepared mustard
4	cloves of garlic, crushed
·	Cream Puffs

Cook the shrimp in boiling water seasoned with the bay leaf and Old Bay seasoning until the shrimp turns pink; drain. Peel and devein the shrimp. Process the shrimp in a food processor until coarsely chopped. Combine with the onion and salt in a bowl and mix well. Beat the cream cheese and mayonnaise in a bowl until smooth. Add the catsup, mustard and garlic and mix well. Fold into the shrimp mixture. Cut the tops from the Cream Puffs and remove the centers. Spoon the shrimp filling into the Cream Puffs and replace the tops. Place on a greased baking sheet. Bake at 350 degrees for 8 to 10 minutes or until heated through. Chill until serving time. May freeze, tightly covered, for up to 1 month, thawing for 1 hour before reheating. Yield: 72 servings.

CREAM PUFFS

1	cup water
1/2	cup butter
1	cup flour, sifted
1/2	teaspoon salt
4	eggs

Bring the water and butter to a boil in a saucepan. Add the flour and salt, stirring constantly until the mixture forms a ball. Let stand until cool. Add the eggs 1 at a time, beating for 1 minute after each addition. Drop by teaspoonfuls 1 inch apart on an ungreased baking sheet. Bake at 425 degrees for 15 to 20 minutes or until golden brown. Cool on wire racks.

Because all three ships stuck in the mud at low tide, this struggle came to be known as "Battle of the Mud Flats." With the eventual surrender of the pirates, Stede Bonnet and thirty others were captured and later hanged on the wharves of White Point in Charleston, South Carolina.

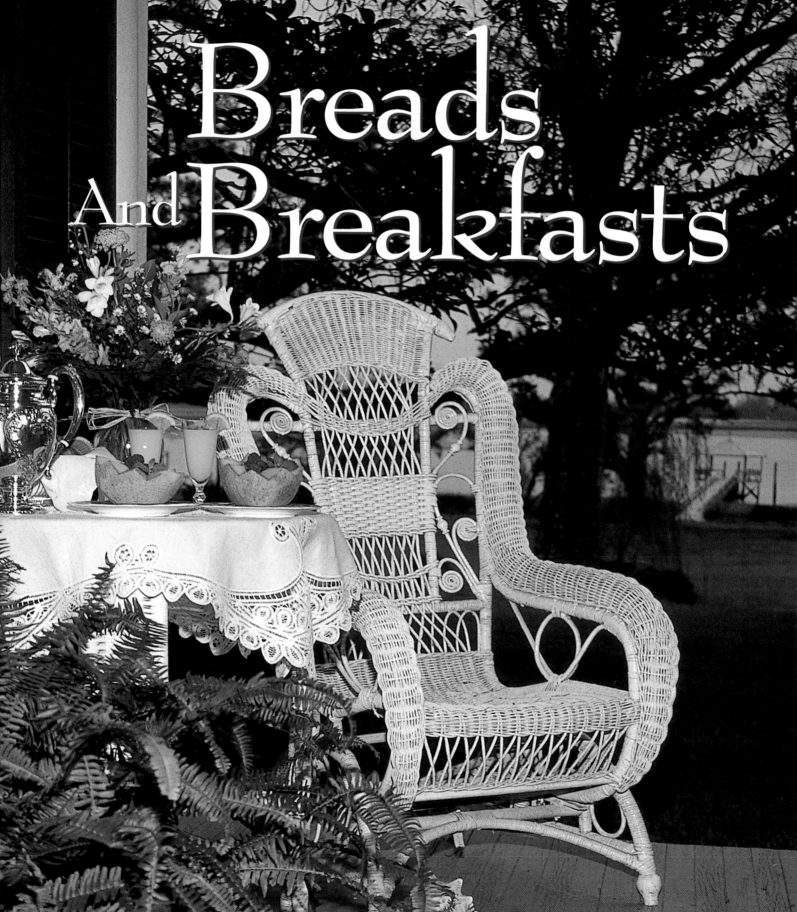

Breads
And Breakfasts

This picturesque setting overlooking the intracoastal waterway sets the tone for a luxurious morning of gracious entertaining. Tourists enjoy many elegant bed and breakfast inns in the heart of the historic district, or relax by the Atlantic Ocean, listening to the sounds of the breakers and frolicking in the sand and surf.

DILL BISCUITS

2	cups flour
1	tablespoon baking powder
1	teaspoon sugar
1	teaspoon salt
2	tablespoons unsalted butter, chilled
3	tablespoons chopped fresh dillweed
1	cup whipping cream
·	Milk

Sift the flour, baking powder, sugar and salt into a bowl. Cut in the butter with a pastry blender until crumbly. Stir in the dillweed. Add the cream, stirring until a soft dough forms. Shape into a ball on a lightly floured surface. Pat into a rectangle 1/2 inch thick. Cut into 2-inch circles. Place on a buttered baking sheet. Brush the tops with milk. Bake at 425 degrees for 15 to 17 minutes or until golden brown. Yield: 8 servings.

ORANGE MARMALADE BISCUITS

A morning favorite, these biscuits are the perfect way to start the day.

2	cups flour
4	teaspoons baking powder
1/2	teaspoon salt
1/4	cup plus 1 tablespoon shortening
1	egg, lightly beaten
1/3	cup milk
1/3	cup orange marmalade

Mix the flour, baking powder and salt in a bowl. Cut in the shortening with a pastry blender until crumbly. Combine the egg, milk and orange marmalade in a bowl and mix well. Add to the flour mixture, stirring just until moistened. Knead 8 to 10 times on a lightly floured surface. Roll the dough into a circle 1/2 inch thick. Cut with a 2-inch biscuit cutter. Place on an ungreased baking sheet. Bake at 450 degrees for 8 to 10 minutes or until golden brown. Yield: 1 1/2 dozen.

CINNAMON AND BROWN SUGAR COFFEE CAKE

2½ cups flour

1   tablespoon baking powder

1   teaspoon baking soda

¼   teaspoon salt

1   cup butter or margarine, softened

1   cup sugar

1   cup sour cream

1   teaspoon vanilla extract

3   eggs

½   cup sugar

½   cup packed brown sugar

3   tablespoons cinnamon

½   cup chopped pecans or walnuts

·   Several drops of milk

Sift the flour, baking powder, baking soda and salt together. Cream the butter and 1 cup sugar in a mixer bowl until light and fluffy. Add the sour cream, vanilla and eggs 1 at a time, beating well after each addition. Beat in the flour mixture. Mix the ½ cup sugar, brown sugar, cinnamon and pecans in a bowl. Place ½ of the batter in a nonstick bundt pan. Layer ⅔ of the pecan mixture, the remaining batter and the remaining pecan mixture in the prepared pan. Press down. Sprinkle the top with the milk. Bake at 350 degrees for 1 hour. Cool for 1 hour before removing from the pan. Yield: 12 servings.

In the 1980s Orton's stately columns and shady live oaks made an attractive backdrop for moviemaker Dino DeLaurentis. He was so intrigued with the area he built a movie studio, giving birth to the burgeoning industry that remains strong today.

ORANGE BLOSSOM BREAKFAST CAKE

1	envelope dry yeast
1/4	cup warm (105 to 115 degrees) water
1/2	cup warm (105 to 115 degrees) milk
1/2	cup fresh orange juice
1/2	cup sugar
1/2	cup ricotta cheese
1	tablespoon grated orange zest
1/2	teaspoon salt
1	large egg, lightly beaten
3 1/2	to 4 cups flour
1	large egg, lightly beaten
·	Orange Icing

Dissolve the yeast in the warm water in a large bowl. Let stand for 5 to 10 minutes or until foamy. Stir in the warm milk, orange juice, sugar, ricotta cheese, orange zest, salt and 1 egg. Add 2 cups of the flour, beating at low speed until a soft dough forms. Beat in the remaining flour 1/2 cup at a time until a stiff dough forms. Knead the dough on a lightly floured surface for 5 to 10 minutes or until smooth and elastic, adding additional flour as needed to prevent sticking. Place the dough in a greased bowl, turning to coat the surface. Cover with a damp cloth. Let rise for 1 1/2 hours. Punch down the dough. Knead on a lightly floured surface for 1 to 2 minutes. Divide the dough into 3 equal portions. Roll each portion into a rope 20 inches long. Braid the ropes together. Coil the braided dough into a greased 10-inch springform pan, tucking the ends under. Cover with a damp cloth and let rise for 30 minutes. Brush the dough with 1 beaten egg. Bake at 425 degrees for 25 to 30 minutes or until golden brown. Invert the coffee cake onto a wire rack to cool slightly. Place on a serving plate. Spread the Orange Icing over the warm coffee cake. Serve warm. Yield: 12 servings.

ORANGE ICING

1	cup confectioners' sugar
1 1/2	to 2 tablespoons fresh orange juice

Beat the confectioners' sugar and orange juice in a small bowl until smooth.

SOUTHWESTERN CORN BREAD

2	eggs
2/3	cup vegetable oil
1	cup sour cream
1	cup yellow cornmeal
3/4	cup yellow cream-style corn
1	tablespoon baking powder
1 1/2	teaspoons salt
2	green onion tops, finely chopped (optional)
4	small jalapeños, seeded, finely chopped (optional)
1	cup shredded Cheddar cheese

Beat the eggs and oil in a bowl. Add the sour cream, cornmeal, corn, baking powder and salt and mix well. Stir in the green onion tops, jalapeños and 1/2 of the cheese. Spread in a greased 8x12-inch baking pan. Cover the top with the remaining cheese. Bake at 425 degrees for 20 to 25 minutes or until the bread tests done. Serve immediately. May fill greased 2 1/2-inch muffin cups 2/3 full and bake at 400 degrees for 20 to 25 minutes or until golden brown for corn bread muffins. May substitute 1/4 cup finely chopped onion for the green onion tops.
Yield: 8 to 10 servings.

PEPPER STICKS

2	cups flour
1	tablespoon baking powder
1/2	teaspoon baking soda
1	teaspoon coarsely cracked black peppercorns
2/3	cup grated Parmesan cheese
3	tablespoons butter or margarine
1	cup buttermilk
2	tablespoons melted butter or margarine

Combine the flour, baking powder, baking soda, cracked peppercorns and Parmesan cheese in a bowl and mix well. Cut in 3 tablespoons butter with a pastry blender until crumbly. Add the buttermilk and stir just until the mixture is moistened. Knead the dough on a lightly floured surface 4 or 5 times. Roll into a 9x12-inch rectangle. Cut into 1 1/2x3-inch rectangles. Place on lightly greased baking sheets. Brush with the melted butter. Bake at 450 degrees for 10 minutes or until light brown. Yield: 2 dozen.

SPICY APPLESAUCE LOAF

2	cups flour
1	teaspoon baking soda
½	teaspoon baking powder
½	teaspoon cinnamon
¼	teaspoon salt
¼	teaspoon allspice
½	teaspoon nutmeg
½	cup applesauce
1	cup sugar
½	cup vegetable oil
2	eggs
3	tablespoons milk
1	cup raisins (optional)
½	cup chopped pecans
½	cup packed brown sugar
¼	cup chopped pecans
½	teaspoon cinnamon

Sift the flour, baking soda, baking powder, ½ teaspoon cinnamon, salt, allspice and nutmeg together. Combine the applesauce, sugar, vegetable oil, eggs and milk in a bowl and mix well. Stir in the raisins. Add the flour mixture and mix well. Stir in ½ cup pecans. Pour into a greased 5x9-inch loaf pan. Sprinkle with a mixture of brown sugar, ¼ cup pecans and ½ teaspoon cinnamon. Bake at 350 degrees for 1 hour or until the loaf tests done. May spoon batter into 12 muffin cups and bake at 400 degrees for 20 minutes or until the muffins test done. May store the bread loaf or muffins in the freezer. Yield: 12 to 15 servings.

STRAWBERRY BREAD

2	(10-ounce) packages frozen strawberries, thawed
4	eggs
1¼	cups vegetable oil
3	cups flour
2	cups sugar
1	tablespoon cinnamon
1	teaspoon baking soda
1	teaspoon salt
1	cup chopped nuts

Process the strawberries in a food processor until puréed. Combine the strawberry purée, eggs and oil in a medium bowl and mix well. Mix the flour, sugar, cinnamon, baking soda, salt and nuts in a large bowl. Add the strawberry mixture and stir just until blended. Pour into 2 greased and floured 5x9-inch loaf pans. Bake at 350 degrees for 1 hour or until the loaves test done. Yield: 24 to 30 servings.

CITRUS BLUEBERRY MUFFINS

Fresh blueberries are a must in this recipe.

3½	cups bread flour
1½	tablespoons baking powder
½	cup shortening
½	cup unsalted butter, softened
1¾	cups sugar
1¾	cups milk
2	tablespoons grated orange zest
¾	tablespoon vanilla extract
1	teaspoon lemon extract
2	cups (heaping) fresh blueberries
2	tablespoons cinnamon-sugar

Mix the bread flour and baking powder in a bowl. Cream the shortening, butter and sugar in a mixer bowl until light and fluffy. Add the flour mixture and milk alternately, beating well after each addition. Stir in the orange zest and flavorings. Fold in the blueberries. Fill nonstick muffin cups full. Sprinkle with the cinnamon-sugar. Bake at 375 degrees for 15 to 20 minutes or until the muffins test done. Yield: 2½ dozen.

When setting sail, the ship Fortuna mysteriously exploded in the harbor. The other two ships escaped. Local citizens recovered the sunken vessel. Most of the contents were sold, with the proceeds going to the construction of Brunswick's church, St. Phillip's, and to Wilmington's St. James Parish that also received "Ecce Homo."

ONION CHEESE MUFFINS

These golden muffins have a special flavor.

1	tablespoon butter or margarine
1/2	cup chopped yellow or white onion
1 1/2	cups flour
2 1/4	teaspoons baking powder
1/4	teaspoon salt
3	tablespoons shortening
1	egg, lightly beaten
1/2	cup milk
1	cup shredded sharp Cheddar cheese
1	tablespoon melted butter or margarine
2	teaspoons poppy seeds or sesame seeds

Melt 1 tablespoon butter in a small skillet. Add the onion. Sauté until transparent. Mix the flour, baking powder and salt in a large bowl. Cut in the shortening with a pastry blender until crumbly. Make a well in the center. Add the egg, milk, onion and 1/2 cup of the cheese. Mix well by hand; do not overmix. Spoon into greased muffin cups. Sprinkle with the remaining 1/2 cup cheese. Drizzle with 1 tablespoon melted butter. Sprinkle with the poppy seeds. Bake at 400 degrees for 12 to 15 minutes or until the muffins test done. May bake in an 8- or 9-inch square or round baking pan for 25 minutes and cut into squares or wedges before serving. Yield: 10 to 12 muffins.

SOUR CREAM MUFFINS

Delicious with morning coffee and simple to prepare.

1/2	cup butter
1	cup sour cream
1/2	cup shredded Cheddar cheese
2	cups self-rising flour

Melt the butter in a large saucepan and remove from the heat. Pour into a mixer bowl. Add the sour cream, cheese and flour and mix well. Fill ungreased 1³/₄-inch miniature muffin cups full. Bake at 350 degrees for 25 minutes or until the muffins test done. May fill regular-size muffin cups half full and bake at 450 degrees for 10 to 12 minutes. Yield: 2 dozen miniature muffins.

CHEESY SAUSAGE MUFFINS

8	ounces bulk pork sausage
·	Melted butter or margarine
1	egg, lightly beaten
1	cup milk
2	cups flour
2	tablespoons sugar
1	tablespoon baking powder
1/4	teaspoon salt
1/2	cup shredded Cheddar cheese

Brown the sausage in a skillet over medium heat, stirring until crumbly. Drain, reserving the drippings. Add enough melted butter to the drippings to measure 1/4 cup. Combine the reserved dripping mixture, egg and milk in a bowl and mix well. Mix the flour, sugar, baking powder and salt in a large bowl. Make a well in the center. Add the egg mixture and mix just until moistened. Stir in the sausage and cheese. The batter will be thick. Fill greased muffin cups 3/4 full. Bake at 375 degrees for 18 to 20 minutes or until the muffins test done. Remove from the muffin cups immediately. May fill greased 1³/₄-inch miniature muffin cups 2/3 full and bake at 400 degrees for 12 to 14 minutes for 2¹/₂ dozen miniature muffins. Yield: 1 dozen.

COUNTRY HAM SCONES

1³⁄₄	cups flour
2	teaspoons baking powder
¹⁄₂	teaspoon salt
¹⁄₄	cup yellow cornmeal
2	tablespoons sugar
¹⁄₄	teaspoon pepper
6	tablespoons butter, cut up
³⁄₄	cup slivered cooked country ham
1	cup whipping cream

Mix the flour, baking powder, salt, cornmeal, sugar and pepper in a large bowl. Cut in the butter until crumbly. Stir in the ham. Add the whipping cream and stir with a fork just until moistened. Knead the dough on a lightly floured surface 3 or 4 times. Pat into a 7-inch circle on a lightly greased baking sheet. Cut into 10 wedges; do not separate. Bake at 425 degrees for 24 to 26 minutes or until the scones are golden brown. Cool slightly. Separate into wedges and serve with butter. Yield: 10 servings.

SALLY LUNN MUFFINS

An English lass, Sally Lunn, popularized this cake-like bread in the eighteenth century. Sally Lunn is listed in the Oxford English Dictionary—hers was a household name in the southern colonies as it was in England. This particular recipe has been passed down through several generations. It is so easy to prepare.

1	envelope dry yeast
1/2	cup lukewarm water
1/2	cup shortening
1/4	cup sugar
4	cups sifted flour
2	eggs
1	teaspoon (or less) salt
1	cup milk

Dissolve the yeast in the lukewarm water. Cream the shortening and sugar in a mixer bowl until light and fluffy. Add 1 cup of the flour and the yeast mixture and mix well. Add the eggs 1 at a time, beating well after each addition. Mix the salt with the remaining flour. Add to the creamed mixture alternately with the milk, beating constantly until smooth. Fill greased muffin cups 1/2 full. Let rise in a warm place until doubled in bulk. Bake at 400 degrees for 12 to 15 minutes or until golden brown. May be frozen and are delicious split and toasted for breakfast. May spoon the dough into a greased 10-inch bundt pan and let rise for 1 hour or until doubled in bulk. Bake at 350 degrees for 40 minutes. Cool in the pan for 10 minutes and invert onto a wire rack to cool. Yield: 20 to 24 servings.

The ship sailed on and the officer swam to shore, where his colonial brother corroborated his patriot leanings. The former Tory joined the Revolutionary Army and served admirably before settling in Wilmington.

BLUE CRAB MEAT OMELETS

12	eggs
1½	teaspoons salt
·	Pepper to taste
¼	cup margarine
1½	cups shredded Cheddar cheese
·	Blue Crab Meat Filling

Combine 2 of the eggs, ¼ teaspoon of the salt and pepper to taste in a bowl and beat well. Melt 2 teaspoons of the margarine in an omelet pan. Heat until the margarine sizzles. Add the egg mixture. Cook until the egg mixture is almost set, running a spatula around the edge and lifting slightly to allow the uncooked egg mixture to flow underneath. Sprinkle with ¼ cup of the cheese. Cook until the cheese melts. Place ½ cup of the Blue Crab Meat Filling on 1 half of the omelet and fold the remaining half over the filling. Remove to a warm platter. Repeat the procedure 5 times with the remaining ingredients. Yield: 6 servings.

BLUE CRAB MEAT FILLING

1	pound blue crab meat, drained, flaked
2	cups half-and-half
2	tablespoons sliced green onions
½	teaspoon thyme
½	teaspoon salt
6	to 8 drops of Tabasco sauce
2	tablespoons flour
¼	cup water

Heat the crab meat, half-and-half, green onions, thyme, salt and Tabasco sauce in a saucepan. Stir in a mixture of the flour and water. Cook until thickened, stirring constantly. Yield: 3 cups.

GARDEN FRITTATA

3	tablespoons butter
1	medium onion, thinly sliced
1	cup sliced peeled potatoes
·	Salt and pepper to taste
1	tablespoon minced fresh basil
2	cups sliced zucchini
1	cup drained, chopped, seeded peeled tomatoes
1/2	cup chopped red bell pepper
1/2	cup chopped green bell pepper
3	tablespoons butter
6	eggs
1/8	teaspoon Tabasco sauce
2	cups shredded Monterey Jack cheese

Melt 3 tablespoons butter in an ovenproof skillet. Add the onion and potatoes. Cook until the vegetables are brown and tender-crisp. Sprinkle with the salt, pepper and basil. Add the zucchini. Cook for 5 minutes. Stir in the tomatoes, red pepper and green pepper. Cook for 10 minutes or until most of the liquid has evaporated. Add 3 tablespoons butter, letting the melted butter run underneath the vegetables. Beat the eggs and Tabasco sauce in a bowl. Pour over the vegetables, lifting the vegetables slightly so the egg mixture can run underneath. Cook for 5 minutes or until the eggs are set. Sprinkle with the cheese. Place on an oven rack under a preheated broiler. Broil until the cheese melts and is bubbly. Remove from the oven. Cool for 5 minutes. Cut into wedges and serve. May use your favorite garden vegetables in this recipe. Yield: 6 servings.

In 1765 Parliament passed the Stamp Act, a law that taxed the colonies without their representation. Nowhere was resistance to this act more pronounced than in Cape Fear. On October 19, 1765, approximately five hundred people gathered near the courthouse at Front and Market and watched as an effigy of Lord Bute, blamed for passage of the Act, burned in a bonfire. The crowd cheered until midnight: "Confusion to Lord Bute and all his adherents!" and "Liberty, Property, and No Stamp Duty," following each toast with three hurrahs.

GREEN CHILE CHEESE BAKE

1	(12-ounce) can evaporated milk
2	tablespoons flour
4	eggs, lightly beaten
1	teaspoon salt
1	pound medium-sharp Cheddar cheese, shredded
1	pound Monterey Jack cheese, shredded
2	(4-ounce) cans chopped green chiles, drained
1	large tomato, sliced

Mix enough of the evaporated milk with the flour in a bowl to form a paste. Stir in the remaining evaporated milk. Add the eggs and salt and mix well. Layer the Cheddar cheese, Monterey Jack cheese and green chiles in a nonstick 9x13-inch shallow baking dish. Pour the egg mixture over the layers. Bake at 325 degrees for 30 minutes. Arrange the sliced tomato over the top. Bake for 15 minutes. Serve warm or at room temperature. Yield: 6 servings.

INDIVIDUAL HAM AND EGG BRUNCH CASSEROLES

1/4	cup butter
1/4	cup flour
1	cup milk
1/2	cup chicken stock
1/2	cup vermouth
·	Salt and pepper to taste
4	slices ham
8	eggs
·	Grated Parmesan cheese to taste

Melt the butter in a saucepan. Stir in the flour until blended. Add the milk, chicken stock and vermouth, stirring constantly. Cook until thickened, stirring constantly. Season with salt and pepper. Remove from the heat. Place 1 slice ham in each of 4 small baking dishes. Break 2 of the eggs over each slice of ham. Pour the sauce over the eggs. Sprinkle with Parmesan cheese. Bake at 400 degrees for 10 to 15 minutes or until the eggs are set. May substitute Canadian bacon for the ham. Yield: 4 servings.

SHRIMP PIE

12	ounces fresh shrimp, rinsed
1	large Vidalia onion, chopped
2	tablespoons extra-virgin olive oil
4	ounces feta cheese, crumbled
4	ounces mozzarella cheese, shredded
4	ounces Cheddar cheese, shredded
1/2	cup chopped fresh cilantro
1/2	cup chopped fresh parsley
1/4	cup chopped fresh chives
1	teaspoon freshly ground black pepper
·	Pastry for Shrimp Pie
·	Chopped dried red pepper to taste

Peel and devein the shrimp. Rinse the peeled shrimp. Chop the shrimp and place in a bowl. Chill, covered, in the refrigerator. Sauté the onion in the olive oil in a skillet until transparent; drain slightly. Mix the feta cheese, mozzarella cheese, Cheddar cheese, cilantro, parsley, chives and black pepper in a large bowl. Divide the Pastry for Shrimp Pie into 2 equal portions. Roll each portion into a 12-inch circle on a lightly floured surface. Fit 1 circle into a large pie plate. Prick the bottom and side with a fork. Add the sautéed onion and shrimp to the cheese mixture and mix well. Sprinkle with red pepper and toss lightly. Spoon into the prepared pie plate. Top with the remaining pastry circle, sealing and fluting the edge and cutting vents. Bake at 425 degrees for 10 minutes. Reduce the oven temperature to 350 degrees. Bake for 20 to 25 minutes longer or until the crust is golden brown. Let stand for 10 minutes before serving. Yield: 8 servings.

PASTRY FOR SHRIMP PIE

2	cups flour
1	teaspoon salt
2/3	cup shortening
1	egg yolk, chilled
3	tablespoons cold water

Sift the flour into a bowl. Add the salt and mix well. Cut in the shortening with a pastry blender until crumbly. Add the egg yolk and water, stirring constantly and adding additional cold water as necessary until the mixture shapes into a ball. Chill, covered, in the refrigerator for 25 minutes.

GWENZY'S CRAB MEAT QUICHE

A recipe tester declared this recipe to be "insanely delicious."

1   unbaked (10-inch) deep-dish pie shell
2   cups drained, flaked backfin crab meat
1/2 cup thinly sliced green onions with tops
1/2 cup evaporated milk
2   tablespoons flour
2   to 3 eggs, beaten
1/2 cup mayonnaise
1   teaspoon Worcestershire sauce
1/4 teaspoon dry mustard
8   ounces Swiss cheese, shredded

Prick the bottom and side of the pie shell with a fork. Bake at 450 degrees for 8 minutes. Remove from the oven. Reduce the oven temperature to 350 degrees. Combine the crab meat and green onions in a large bowl. Mix the evaporated milk and flour in a bowl until smooth. Beat in the eggs. Add a mixture of the mayonnaise, Worcestershire sauce and dry mustard and beat for a few seconds. Stir into the crab meat mixture. Add the cheese and mix well. Pour into the prebaked pie shell. Place on a baking sheet. Bake for 45 minutes or until firm. Yield: 6 to 8 servings.

SPINACH QUICHE

1   (10-ounce) package frozen chopped spinach

1½   cups sliced mushrooms

1½   cups sliced zucchini

¾   cup chopped green bell pepper

¾   cup chopped onion

1½   teaspoons minced garlic

3   tablespoons vegetable oil

5   eggs

16   ounces ricotta cheese

1   tablespoon chopped fresh parsley

1½   teaspoons chopped fresh thyme

¾   teaspoon salt

¼   teaspoon freshly ground pepper

7   ounces feta cheese, crumbled

·   Hard-cooked egg slices

·   Paprika to taste

·   Yellow cherry tomatoes

Thaw the spinach and drain well. Cover the spinach with paper towels and squeeze out any additional moisture. Sauté the mushrooms, zucchini, green pepper, onion and garlic in the vegetable oil in a skillet until tender-crisp; drain. Let stand until cool. Beat the eggs and ricotta cheese in a bowl until blended. Stir in the sautéed vegetables, parsley, thyme, salt, pepper, feta cheese and drained spinach. Pour into a lightly greased 10-inch springform pan. Bake at 350 degrees for 1 hour or until set. Cool for 10 minutes. Remove the side of the pan. Garnish with hard-cooked egg slices, paprika and yellow cherry tomatoes. Yield: 6 to 8 servings.

On November 16, 1765, a mob of approximately four hundred people marched to beating drums to the lodging of the newly appointed stamp master, Mr. William Houston, Esq., and demanded to know if he intended to execute his onerous duty. Mr. Houston resigned his post on the spot to the delight of the crowd, and they carried him around the courthouse in a chair, cheering him at every corner. That night these Sons of Liberty made a bonfire and drank all the favorite American toasts. Everyone on the streets sported the word "Liberty" on their hats.

VEGETABLE QUICHES

1	small package chopped fresh mushrooms
1	onion, chopped
3/4	green bell pepper, chopped
·	Vegetable oil for sautéing
4	eggs, beaten
7	ounces half-and-half
6	ounces Cheddar cheese, shredded
6	ounces mozzarella cheese, shredded
2	unbaked (9-inch) pie shells

Sauté the mushrooms, onion and green pepper in a small amount of vegetable oil until tender. Combine the eggs and half-and-half in a large bowl and mix well. Stir in the sautéed vegetables, Cheddar cheese and mozzarella cheese. Pour into the pie shells. Bake at 350 degrees for 35 to 45 minutes or until the top is golden brown and the center is firm. Let cool for 10 minutes before serving. Yield: 12 to 16 servings.

SWEET POTATO AND PECAN WAFFLES

1 tablespoon vegetable oil

1 small sweet potato

1¼ cups milk

1 large egg

1½ tablespoons melted unsalted butter

1 cup flour

1 tablespoon light brown sugar

1 teaspoon baking powder

¼ teaspoon salt

⅓ cup coarsely chopped pecans

Rub the vegetable oil on the skin of the sweet potato. Bake at 350 degrees for 1 hour or until tender. Let stand until cool. Peel the sweet potato and place the pulp in a bowl; mash well. Add the milk, egg and butter and mix well. Mix the flour, brown sugar, baking powder and salt in a large mixer bowl. Add the sweet potato mixture and mix gently; do not overmix. The batter should be lumpy. Stir in the pecans. Ladle the batter onto a hot waffle iron, sprinkling with additional chopped pecans if desired. Bake until brown using the manufacturer's directions. Serve warm with butter or syrup. May wrap cooled waffles individually in foil and store in the freezer. To reheat, unwrap and place on an ungreased baking sheet. Bake at 400 degrees for 8 to 10 minutes or until heated through. May substitute ¾ cup canned sweet potatoes for the fresh. Yield: 4 (2-waffle) servings.

STRAWBERRY BUTTER

Serve with warm biscuits, toasted Sally Lunn or use as a spread on toast points, fruit breads or pound cake.

1 cup sliced fresh strawberries

1 cup unsalted butter, softened

½ cup confectioners' sugar

Combine the strawberries, butter and confectioners' sugar in a bowl and mix well. Store, covered, in the refrigerator. Yield: 1¾ cups.

BLOODY MARY COCKTAILS

1	(32-ounce) bottle Clamato juice, chilled
15	drops of Tabasco sauce
3	tablespoons Worcestershire sauce
3	pinches celery salt
1/4	teaspoon prepared horseradish
·	Salt and pepper to taste
·	Juice of 1/8 lime
·	Vodka to taste
4	cucumber sticks
4	celery sticks

Combine the Clamato juice, Tabasco sauce, Worcestershire sauce, celery salt, horseradish, salt, pepper, lime juice and vodka in a serving pitcher and mix well. Pour into individual glasses. Garnish each serving with a cucumber stick and celery stick. Yield: 4 servings.

SPICED FRUIT JUICE

2 1/2	cups orange juice
1 1/2	teaspoons grated lemon peel
3	tablespoons lemon juice
1	cup pineapple juice
2	cups water
6	whole cloves
1/2	cup sugar
1	tablespoon honey
1/2	teaspoon nutmeg
1/2	teaspoon cinnamon
1/4	teaspoon allspice
·	Cracked ice
1 1/2	quarts ginger ale

Combine the orange juice, lemon peel, lemon juice, pineapple juice, water, cloves, sugar, honey, nutmeg, cinnamon and allspice in a large pitcher and mix well. Let stand, covered, in a warm place for 3 hours. Strain the juice mixture over cracked ice in a punch bowl. Add the ginger ale. Ladle into punch cups. Yield: 24 servings.

Mimosa Hawaiian

1	(12-ounce) can apricot nectar
1	(12-ounce) can pineapple juice
1	(6-ounce) can frozen orange juice concentrate, thawed
¾	cup water
1	(25.4-ounce) bottle white Champagne, chilled

Mix the apricot nectar, pineapple juice, orange juice concentrate and water in a large pitcher. Chill in the refrigerator. Stir in the Champagne. Serve immediately. Yield: 7½ cups.

Coffee Smoothie

1	quart whipping cream
5	tablespoons sugar
5	teaspoons vanilla extract
2	quarts vanilla or chocolate ice cream
1	gallon strong brewed coffee, chilled

Whip the whipping cream in a bowl until soft peaks form. Beat in the sugar and vanilla. Place the ice cream and whipped cream in a punch bowl. Pour the coffee over the top and mix well. Ladle into punch cups. Cut the ice cream into thin slices if block ice cream is used. Yield: 50 to 60 servings.

Coffee Shakes

5	cups vanilla or chocolate ice cream
1	cup brewed coffee, chilled
1	teaspoon vanilla extract
·	Nutmeg to taste
·	Cinnamon to taste

Process the ice cream, coffee and vanilla in a blender until smooth. Pour into individual serving glasses. Sprinkle with nutmeg and cinnamon. Yield: 6 servings.

After the war, prosperity returned, along with festive celebrations that marked the area. From his plantation on the Cape Fear River, Alfred Moore wrote on December 14, 1786: "There have been three grand balls, and two horse races at this place within a week: and at this moment five fiddles are playing a lively tune and the whole town are (sic) dancing to it."

Soups
And Salads

*Cape Fear Alfresco—
A beautiful evening sets the
stage for enjoying a delicious
soup-and-salad meal.
The recipes are a sure success
for an evening indoors or out.
When the cold winter winds
have you longing for the sunny
shore, invite friends over for
Hearty Fish Gumbo—perfect
for casually entertaining a
crowd. Try serving the Oyster
and Artichoke Soup as a first
course to whet everyone's
appetite for the feast to come.*

CAULIFLOWER SOUP

Deceptively mild and brimming with flavor, this soup can be served as a meal by itself.

5	cups cauliflowerets
3	cups chicken broth
2	tablespoons low-fat cream cheese
1/2	cup finely chopped carrot
1/2	cup finely chopped celery
1/2	cup sliced scallions
1	tablespoon Spike seasoning
1	teaspoon Louisiana hot sauce
·	Pepper to taste
1/2	cup fresh or frozen peas

Combine the cauliflowerets and chicken broth in a stockpot. Cook over medium heat for 20 minutes or until the cauliflowerets are tender-crisp. Pour into a blender container and add the cream cheese. Purée until smooth, adding additional chicken broth if needed for the desired consistency. Return to the stockpot. Add the carrot, celery, scallions, Spike seasoning, hot sauce and pepper. Cook over low heat for 5 to 10 minutes or until the vegetables are tender. Stir in the peas. Cook until the peas are tender. Ladle into soup bowls. Yield: 4 to 6 servings.

GAZPACHO

1	cucumber
1	(46-ounce) can tomato juice
2	(16-ounce) cans chopped peeled tomatoes with basil
1/2	cup chopped celery
1	green bell pepper, chopped
1/4	red bell pepper, chopped
1 1/2	bunches green onions, chopped
2	cloves of garlic, minced (optional)
1/2	cup red wine vinegar
1/4	cup extra-virgin olive oil
2	tablespoons fresh lemon juice
1	tablespoon Worcestershire sauce
1	to 2 teaspoons sugar
1/4	teaspoon cumin
·	Freshly ground pepper to taste
·	Several drops of Tabasco sauce
·	Sprigs of cilantro

Peel the cucumber. Cut into 8 slices and discard the seeds from the centers. Combine the cucumber, tomato juice, undrained tomatoes, celery, green bell pepper, red bell pepper, green onions, garlic, vinegar, olive oil, lemon juice, Worcestershire sauce, sugar, cumin, ground pepper and Tabasco sauce in a large bowl and mix well. Chill, covered, in the refrigerator. Ladle into serving bowls. Garnish each serving with sprigs of cilantro. May use 6 to 8 fresh large tomatoes, peeled, seeded and chopped, instead of the canned tomatoes and 1 large onion, chopped, instead of the green onions. Yield: 8 (6-ounce) servings.

CAROLINA ONION SOUP

14   to 18 medium onions, coarsely chopped
¼   cup olive oil
¼   cup unsalted butter
·   Salt and pepper to taste
2   tablespoons sugar
8   cups beef broth
8   slices French bread
½   cup freshly grated Parmesan cheese

Sauté the onions in the olive oil in a large skillet for 15 to 20 minutes or until the onions are translucent. Add the butter, salt, pepper and sugar and mix well. Heat the beef broth in a large saucepan. Stir in the onions. Trim the bread to fit individual ovenproof earthenware cups. Toast the bread lightly. Place a bread slice in each cup. Ladle the soup into the cups. Sprinkle each serving with 1 tablespoon cheese. Bake, covered, at 375 degrees for 20 minutes. Serve immediately. May substitute peanut oil for the olive oil. Yield: 8 servings.

BAKED POTATO SOUP

1	cup chopped celery
1	cup chopped onion
2	tablespoons butter
2	tablespoons flour
2	cups half-and-half
1/2	cup water
1	tablespoon chopped fresh parsley
1	teaspoon instant chicken bouillon
1/2	teaspoon salt
1/2	teaspoon pepper
4	large baking potatoes, baked, cubed
·	Grated Cheddar cheese
·	Sour cream
·	Chopped chives
·	Cooked bacon slices, crumbled

Sauté the celery and onion in the butter in a large skillet. Blend the flour with 1/2 cup of the half-and-half in a bowl. Add to the sautéed vegetables. Bring just to a simmer; do not boil. Add the remaining half-and-half, water, parsley, instant bouillon, salt and pepper and mix well. Stir in the potatoes. Cook until heated through; do not boil. Ladle into soup bowls. Garnish with grated Cheddar cheese, sour cream, chopped chives and crumbled bacon. Yield: 2 to 4 servings.

AUNT PITTYPAT'S VEGETABLE SOUP

2	pounds lean stew beef, cut into bite-size pieces
1	tablespoon salt
3	quarts water
1	onion, chopped
1/4	teaspoon thyme
1/4	teaspoon oregano
2	bay leaves
6	to 8 carrots, sliced
1	(28-ounce) can tomato purée
1/2	(10-ounce) package frozen lima beans
1/2	(10-ounce) package cut green beans
1/2	(10-ounce) package green peas
1/2	(10-ounce) package corn kernels
2	tablespoons chopped parsley
1	(6-ounce) can tomato paste
1	teaspoon salt
1/2	teaspoon pepper
4	to 5 small red potatoes, peeled, chopped

Place the beef, 1 tablespoon salt and water in a large stockpot. Cover and bring to a boil. Skim the surface. Add the onion, thyme, oregano and bay leaves. Cook for a few minutes. Add the carrots and tomato purée. Return to a boil and reduce the heat. Simmer for 30 minutes. Add the lima beans, green beans, peas, corn, parsley, tomato paste, 1 teaspoon salt and pepper and mix well. Simmer, covered, for 2 hours. Add the potatoes. Simmer for 1 1/2 hours. Let stand until cool. Chill, covered, for several hours before serving to enhance the flavors. Discard the bay leaves. Reheat the soup and serve with French bread. Yield: 8 to 10 servings.

WILD RICE SOUP

1	large onion, chopped
1	cup chopped celery
4	ounces chopped mushrooms
3/4	cup butter or margarine
1	cup flour
1	cup wild rice, cooked
8	cups water
9	chicken bouillon cubes
1	cup whipping cream
·	Chopped fresh parsley

Sauté the onion, celery and mushrooms in the butter in a skillet until tender. Sprinkle with the flour until the vegetables are well coated; the mixture will be pasty. Combine the cooked wild rice, water, bouillon cubes, vegetable mixture and whipping cream in a stockpot. Cook until heated through, stirring constantly; do not boil. Ladle into warm soup bowls and sprinkle with chopped parsley.
Yield: 6 to 8 servings.

Tradition has it that Cornwallis used the dungeon under the basement to hold some patriots during his raids in the Cape Fear region, before his final defeat at Yorktown. Appropriately, since 1937 the Burgwin-Wright House has been the headquarters for the North Carolina Chapter of the National Society of the Colonial Dames of America.

BLACK BEAN CHICKEN CHILI

3/4	cup 1-inch boneless, skinless chicken pieces
1	cup chopped onion
1	cup chopped green bell pepper
2	cloves of garlic, minced
2	tablespoons skimmed broth or bouillon
2	(28-ounce) cans stewed tomatoes
2	(15-ounce) cans black beans, rinsed, drained
1	teaspoon salt
1/2	teaspoon (or more) Louisiana hot sauce
2	cups medium salsa
2	tablespoons chili powder
1	teaspoon cumin

Sauté the chicken, onion, green pepper and garlic in the broth in a stockpot until the chicken is cooked through. Add the tomatoes, black beans, salt, hot sauce, salsa, chili powder and cumin and mix well. Simmer for 30 to 45 minutes. May serve with shredded low-fat cheese. Yield: 8 servings.

BRUNSWICK STEW

4	pounds chicken breasts
2	pounds beef
2	pounds pork
3	quarts tomatoes
2	quarts lima beans
2	cups chopped onions
3	tablespoons Worcestershire sauce
1¼	teaspoons Tabasco sauce, or to taste
·	Salt and pepper to taste
6	potatoes, cubed
2	quarts fresh corn kernels
1	cup butter, sliced
¼	cup flour

Cook the chicken breasts in water to cover in a saucepan until tender and cooked through. Cook the beef in water to cover in a saucepan until tender. Cook the pork in water to cover in a saucepan until cooked through. Drain the chicken, beef and pork, reserving the broths. Shred or chop the chicken, beef and pork, discarding the skin and bones. Combine the chicken, beef, pork, reserved broths, tomatoes, lima beans, onions, Worcestershire sauce, Tabasco sauce, salt and pepper in a large stockpot. Simmer for 2 to 3 hours or longer. Add the potatoes and corn. Cook until the potatoes are nearly tender, stirring frequently to prevent scorching. Roll the butter slices in the flour. Add to the stockpot. Cook for 10 minutes, stirring frequently. Yield: 20 to 25 servings.

OYSTER AND ARTICHOKE SOUP

2	(14-ounce) cans artichokes
1/4	cup butter
1 1/2	cups chopped green onions
2	cloves of garlic, minced
3	tablespoons flour
3	cups chicken broth or stock
3	cups milk
1	teaspoon crushed red pepper
1	teaspoon salt
1/2	teaspoon anise seeds
1	quart oysters
·	Lemon slices

Drain the artichokes and rinse well. Cut into quarters. Melt the butter in a large stockpot. Add the green onions and garlic. Sauté for 5 minutes. Stir in the flour. Cook for 5 minutes, stirring constantly. Add the artichokes, chicken broth, milk, red pepper, salt and anise seeds. Cook for 20 minutes. Add the undrained oysters. Simmer for 10 minutes. Garnish with lemon slices. Yield: 12 servings.

LOW COUNTRY CRAB MEAT STEW

1/2	cup butter
1	small green bell pepper, grated
1	potato, grated
1/4	Vidalia onion, grated
2	cups milk
1	cup half-and-half
1	pound lump crab meat, drained, flaked
·	Salt and pepper to taste
1/8	teaspoon Tabasco sauce
1/8	teaspoon sherry

Melt the butter in a saucepan. Add the green pepper, potato and onion. Cook until the potato is tender. Add the milk and half-and-half. Bring just to a simmer; do not boil. Simmer for a few minutes. Fold in the crab meat. Remove from the heat. Add salt and pepper to taste, Tabasco sauce and sherry. Ladle into soup bowls. May substitute 1 quart stewing oysters, cooked, for the crab meat. May use 1/4 green onion instead of the Vidalia onion. Yield: 2 to 4 servings.

HEARTY FISH GUMBO

Serve as a meal in itself with French bread.

1/4	cup flour	2	ribs celery, chopped
2	cloves of garlic, crushed	4	scallions, chopped
2	teaspoons olive oil	1	green bell pepper, chopped
1/4	cup lemon juice	4	medium potatoes, chopped,
1	(28-ounce) can chopped		or 2/3 cup uncooked rice
	tomatoes	8	ounces mushrooms, sliced
1	teaspoon basil	1	(15-ounce) can black
1	teaspoon rosemary		beans, drained
1/4	teaspoon celery seeds	1	pound okra, sliced
1	teaspoon parsley	2	pounds grouper, king
1	tablespoon salt		mackerel, flounder, drum
1/2	teaspoon thyme		or triggerfish, cut into
8	cups water		bite-size pieces
4	beef bouillon cubes	1	pound shrimp, peeled
4	chicken bouillon cubes	·	Tabasco sauce to taste
1/4	cup extra-dry vermouth	·	Freshly cracked
3	carrots, chopped		peppercorns to taste
2	bay leaves		

Cook the flour and garlic in the olive oil in a 5-quart stockpot over medium-low heat to form a roux, stirring constantly. Reduce the heat to low. Add the lemon juice, tomatoes, basil, rosemary, celery seeds, parsley, salt, thyme, water, beef bouillon cubes, chicken bouillon cubes, vermouth, carrots, bay leaves, celery, scallions, green pepper, potatoes, mushrooms and black beans. Simmer over low heat for 2 hours, stirring occasionally. Add the okra. Cook for 5 minutes. Add the fish and shrimp. Cook for 5 minutes or until the fish is opaque and the shrimp turns pink. Do not overcook. Stir in Tabasco sauce and pepper. Discard the bay leaves. Serve immediately. Yield: 20 (1-cup) servings.

Greatly disturbed by this, Alexander and a friend, Louis Toomer, exhumed Samuel's coffin from St. James Churchyard. To their horror they found one side of the coffin loosened and Samuel's body lying face down, the inside of the coffin and his burial clothes ripped to shreds.

TORTILLA STEW

This is a delicious and colorful stew to serve in the wintertime, especially after the holidays when leftover turkey is abundant and everyone wants something a little different.

2	cups reduced-fat chicken broth
2	cups chopped tomatoes
1/2	cup minced onion
4	jalapeños, seeded, minced
1/2	teaspoon cumin
1/2	teaspoon chili powder
1 1/2	cups chopped cooked turkey breast
2	tablespoons lime juice
2	cups frozen corn
2/3	cup brown rice, cooked
1	cup shredded Monterey Jack cheese
1/4	cup crushed tortilla chips

Combine the broth, tomatoes, onion, jalapeños, cumin and chili powder in a 3-quart saucepan. Bring to a boil and reduce the heat. Simmer for 10 minutes. Stir in the turkey, lime juice, corn and rice. Simmer for 5 minutes or until heated through. Ladle into soup bowls. Sprinkle with the cheese and tortilla chips. Yield: 4 to 6 servings.

POLYNESIAN CHICKEN SALAD

2½ to 3 cups chopped cooked chicken breasts
1   cup finely chopped celery
2   tablespoons finely chopped onion
1   tablespoon finely chopped green bell pepper
1   tablespoon salt, or to taste
½   cup mayonnaise
½   cup slivered almonds, lightly toasted
10   ounces green seedless grapes, cut into halves
1   (9-ounce) can pineapple chunks, drained
2   tablespoons lemon juice

Combine the chicken, celery, onion, green pepper, salt and mayonnaise in a bowl and mix well. Stir in the almonds, grapes, pineapple and lemon juice. Serve on lettuce-lined serving plates or spoon the mixture onto individual pineapple rings. Yield: 4 servings.

GROUPER SALAD

1½ to 2 pounds grouper
1   cup minced celery
½   cup minced onion
¼   cup mayonnaise
1   tablespoon cumin
·   Juice of 1 lemon
1   teaspoon sugar
1   tablespoon paprika
·   Salt and pepper to taste
½   head lettuce, shredded
1   ripe tomato, diced
·   Cherry tomatoes
·   Lemon and lime wedges

Poach the fish in hot water in a saucepan until opaque; drain. Flake the fish, discarding the skin and bones. Combine the fish, celery, onion, mayonnaise, cumin, lemon juice, sugar, paprika, salt and pepper in a bowl and mix until the mixture can be shaped into a mound. Layer the shredded lettuce, fish mixture and tomato on a serving platter. Garnish with cherry tomatoes and lemon and lime wedges. May serve with a vinaigrette salad dressing. Yield: 4 to 6 servings.

In 1733 the town of New Carthage was established, changing its name in 1734 to New Liverpool, and in 1735 to New Town/Newton. When incorporated in 1739–40, the town was renamed Wilmington to honor Spencer Compton, Earl of Wilmington. The culture of the town was enhanced by the founding of the Cape Fear Library in the 1760s. While inland towns struggled with poor roads, Wilmington's access to the river and the sea allowed ease of trade and communication. Travel abroad brought many influences to Wilmington in the areas of its architecture and cosmopolitan culture.

►

ASPIC-TOPPED CRAB MEAT SALAD

Serve for brunch, lunch or a light supper.

1	envelope unflavored gelatin
1/2	cup cold water
3	cups tomato juice cocktail
2	teaspoons Worcestershire sauce
1/4	teaspoon pepper
1/8	teaspoon Tabasco sauce
1	envelope unflavored gelatin
1/4	cup cold water
1 1/2	cups finely chopped celery
1/4	cup finely chopped onion
1	cup mayonnaise
1	cup whipping cream, whipped
3	cups flaked cooked crab meat

Sprinkle 1 envelope gelatin over 1/2 cup cold water in a small saucepan. Let stand for 1 minute. Stir in the tomato juice cocktail. Heat for 1 minute or until the gelatin is dissolved, stirring constantly. Remove from the heat. Stir in the Worcestershire sauce, pepper and Tabasco sauce. Pour into a lightly oiled 11-cup ring mold. Chill until partially set. Sprinkle 1 envelope gelatin over 1/4 cup cold water in a small saucepan. Let stand for 1 minute. Heat over medium heat until the gelatin is dissolved, stirring constantly. Remove from the heat. Let stand until cool. Stir in the celery, onion and mayonnaise. Fold into the whipped cream in a bowl. Fold in the crab meat. Spoon over the partially set layer. Chill until firm. Invert and unmold onto a curly-lettuce-lined serving platter. May substitute chopped cooked chicken for the crab meat. Yield: 8 servings.

SHRIMP SALAD

5	cups water
1	cup white wine or water
15	black peppercorns
1½	tablespoons salt
1½	pounds medium unpeeled shrimp
1	egg yolk
2	tablespoons vegetable oil
2	tablespoons chopped fresh parsley
¼	cup finely grated horseradish
1½	teaspoons fresh lemon juice
1	tablespoon Creole mustard
1	tablespoon catsup
1	tablespoon Worcestershire sauce
1½	teaspoons Tabasco sauce
1	teaspoon paprika
½	teaspoon salt
2	bunches fresh spinach, torn
1	cup chopped celery
1	green bell pepper, chopped
1	medium onion, chopped

Bring the water, wine, peppercorns and 1½ tablespoons salt to a boil in a large stockpot. Add the shrimp. Return to a boil and reduce the heat. Simmer for 5 minutes. Drain the shrimp immediately and plunge into ice water. Peel and devein the shrimp under cold running water. Chill, covered, in the refrigerator.

Process the egg yolk in a blender for 2 minutes. Add the oil in a fine stream, processing constantly. Add the parsley, horseradish, lemon juice, mustard, catsup, Worcestershire sauce, Tabasco sauce, paprika and ½ teaspoon salt 1 at a time, processing well after each addition. Chill, covered, in the refrigerator.

Arrange the spinach on individual salad plates. Combine the chilled shrimp, chilled sauce, celery, green pepper and onion in a large bowl and mix gently. Spoon onto the prepared plates. May use 1 small head Bibb lettuce per serving instead of the spinach. Yield: 6 servings.

The Revolutionary War left the thriving port of Brunswick Town deserted. It had been burned by the British in 1776. Wilmington then became the premier port on the North Carolina coast. The state led the world in the export of naval stores, bringing Wilmington the greatest concentration of wealth of any region in the state in the eighteenth century. The once-bustling port of Brunswick was eventually sold in 1842 to the owner of Orton Plantation for four dollars and twenty-five cents.

MOCK CAESAR SALAD

1	clove of garlic	2	cups firmly packed torn romaine
1/4	cup water	2	tablespoons freshly grated Parmesan cheese
1/8	teaspoon salt		
1	tablespoon white wine vinegar	2	tablespoons pine nuts, toasted
1/2	teaspoon Dijon mustard	1/8	teaspoon freshly ground pepper
1/4	cup olive oil		

Bring the garlic and water to a boil in a small saucepan. Cover and reduce the heat. Simmer for 10 minutes or until soft; drain. Mash the garlic and salt in a salad bowl. Whisk in the vinegar and mustard. Add the olive oil in a fine steady stream, whisking constantly. Add the romaine and toss gently. Sprinkle with the Parmesan cheese, pine nuts and pepper. Yield: 2 servings.

CORN BREAD SALAD

1½	cups bite-size corn bread pieces	1/2	cup each chopped red onion, yellow tomato, red tomato, radishes, cucumber and yellow bell pepper
1	tablespoon olive oil		
1	tablespoon chopped parsley		
1	tablespoon chopped chives	1	ear of fresh corn, roasted, kernels cut from the cob
2	tablespoons balsamic vinegar	1	Anaheim pepper, seeded, chopped
1	tablespoon Dijon mustard	1/2	to 1 cup mozzarella cheese cubes
5	tablespoons olive oil		
2	cups salad greens	·	Salt and pepper to taste

Toss the corn bread pieces with 1 tablespoon olive oil, parsley and chives in a bowl. Place on a baking sheet. Bake at 350 degrees for 10 to 15 minutes or until toasted. Combine the vinegar and mustard in a bowl. Whisk in the 5 tablespoons olive oil. Combine the salad greens, vegetables, corn bread and cheese in a large salad bowl. Add the vinaigrette and toss well. Season with salt and pepper to taste. Serve immediately. May marinate the vegetables in the vinaigrette for 24 hours before serving. Toss with the salad greens, corn bread and cheese just before serving. Yield: 4 to 6 servings.

CUCUMBERS IN SOUR CREAM

2	medium cucumbers	1	tablespoon minced fresh
3/4	cup sour cream		dillweed
1	tablespoon tarragon	1/4	teaspoon salt
	vinegar	1/8	teaspoon pepper
1	tablespoon lemon juice		

Peel the cucumbers and cut into 1/4-inch-thick slices. Blend the sour cream, vinegar, lemon juice, dillweed, salt and pepper in a bowl. Add the cucumbers and toss to mix. Spoon into a serving bowl. Chill, covered, for 1 to 2 hours. Toss before serving. Yield: 4 servings.

CUCUMBER MOUSSE

Serve this delicious summertime salad with seafood, marinated tomatoes and cucumber slices.

5	medium cucumbers	1/8	teaspoon MSG
2	cups water	1/8	teaspoon Tabasco sauce
2	tablespoons lemon juice	1	cup mayonnaise
4	green onions with tops	3	envelopes unflavored
1/2	cup parsley leaves		gelatin
4	teaspoons Worcestershire	1/4	cup cold water
	sauce	1	cup whipping cream,
1 1/2 to 2	teaspoons salt		whipped
1/4	teaspoon pepper		

Peel the cucumbers. Cut into halves lengthwise. Remove the seeds by running a spoon down the middle of each half. Cook the cucumbers in 2 cups water and lemon juice in a saucepan for 20 minutes or until tender; drain well. Process the drained cucumbers, green onions and parsley leaves in a blender until a few specks of green remain. Add the Worcestershire sauce, salt, pepper, MSG, Tabasco sauce and mayonnaise and blend well. Soften the gelatin in 1/4 cup cold water in a saucepan. Heat until the gelatin is dissolved, stirring constantly. Stir into the cucumber mixture in a bowl. Chill until the mixture mounds on a spoon. Fold in the whipped cream. Adjust the seasonings. Pour into a 6-cup ring mold. Chill for 8 to 10 hours. Unmold onto a salad plate. May fill the center with tomato wedges, seafood or additional cucumber slices marinated in French salad dressing. Yield: 8 servings.

BOMBAY ASPIC

Excellent served with fowl.

1   (16-ounce) can sliced peaches
1   (3-ounce) package lemon gelatin
1   cup hot water
1/2 cup (about) chutney

Drain the peaches, reserving 3/4 cup of the syrup. Dissolve the lemon gelatin in the hot water in a bowl. Stir in the reserved peach syrup. Stir in the peaches and chutney. Pour into a serving bowl. Chill until set. Yield: 4 to 6 servings.

EASTER EGG SALAD

2   envelopes unflavored gelatin
1/2 cup cold water
1/2 cup sugar
1   teaspoon salt, or to taste
2   cups hot water
1/2 cup white wine vinegar
2   tablespoons lemon juice
8   seasoned deviled egg halves
1/2 cup finely chopped parsley
1   teaspoon chopped chives

Soften the gelatin in the cold water in a saucepan. Add the sugar, salt and hot water. Heat until the gelatin is dissolved, stirring constantly. Stir in the vinegar and lemon juice. Chill until partially set. Spoon 2 tablespoons of the gelatin mixture into 8 individual scalloped or oval 1-inch-high salad molds. Place a deviled egg half in each mold. Spoon 2 tablespoons of the gelatin mixture around each egg. Sprinkle the eggs with parsley and chives. Fill each mold with the remaining gelatin. Chill until set. Unmold onto individual lettuce-lined salad plates. May be prepared in a ring mold, placing the deviled eggs upside down in the ring. Yield: 8 servings.

FIESTA SALAD

1 1/2	cups mayonnaise
1	(7-ounce) can green chile salsa
1/3	cup catsup
1/2	teaspoon chili powder
1	to 2 heads romaine, torn into 1/2-inch pieces
·	Flour Tortilla Shells
2	(2-ounce) cans sliced black olives
2	to 3 large tomatoes, chopped
1	large red onion, chopped
1/2	cup shredded sharp Cheddar cheese
1	(4-ounce) can chopped green chiles
1	to 2 (6-ounce) packages tortilla chips, crumbled
2	avocados, chopped

Mix the mayonnaise, salsa, catsup and chili powder in a bowl. Chill in the refrigerator. Place the romaine in the Flour Tortilla Shells. Layer each with olives, tomatoes, onion, cheese and green chiles. Sprinkle with the tortilla chips and avocados. Spread the dressing over the tops. Serve immediately. May omit the olives and avocados. Yield: 8 servings.

FLOUR TORTILLA SHELLS

8	(12- or 16-inch) flour tortillas
·	Melted butter

Brush both sides of the tortillas with melted butter. Press each tortilla into a small ovenproof bowl, forming a shell. Bake at 375 degrees for 5 to 8 minutes. Unmold the tortilla shells. Place on the oven rack. Bake for 1 to 2 minutes or until crisp and toasted.

GREEK SALAD WITH HERB VINAIGRETTE

2	heads romaine
3	large ripe tomatoes, cut up
1	cucumber, sliced
1	medium green bell pepper, chopped
1	small red or yellow onion, cut into rings
8	pitted black olives
·	Herb Vinaigrette
2/3	cup crumbled feta cheese

Tear the romaine into large pieces and place in a salad bowl. Add the tomatoes, cucumber, green pepper, onion and black olives and toss well. Add the Herb Vinaigrette and feta cheese and toss well. Serve immediately. Yield: 6 servings.

HERB VINAIGRETTE

5	tablespoons olive oil
1/4	cup red wine vinegar
1	to 2 sprigs of fresh oregano, chopped
1	to 2 sprigs of fresh mint, chopped
3	to 4 sprigs of fresh flat-leaf parsley, chopped
1/2	teaspoon salt
1/4	teaspoon freshly ground pepper

Whisk the olive oil and vinegar in a bowl. Add the oregano, mint, parsley, salt and pepper and whisk well. May substitute dried herbs for the fresh, but use 1/2 to 1/3 less of the dried herb.

Like most other colonial-era cities of note, Wilmington once hosted a visit by the first president of the United States. Enthusiastic crowds gathered on April 24, 1791, to await the arrival of George Washington. The president traveled in style, riding in a white four-horse carriage complete with glass windows and venetian blinds. The townsfolk greeted him with a proper fifteen-gun salute. The following day was filled with festivities and ended with a grand ball held at the assembly hall on Front Street. Washington was overwhelmed by the number of beautiful women who wished to dance with him.

▶

Feta Pear Salad

4	or 5 firm pears
3	lemons
3	tablespoons honey
1/2	cup olive oil
1/2	teaspoon salt
1/8	teaspoon pepper
1	head romaine, torn
1	cup walnut halves
1	cup crumbled feta cheese

Peel the pears and cut into quarters into a bowl. Sprinkle with the juice of 1 of the lemons. Whisk the juice from the remaining lemons, honey, olive oil, salt and pepper in a bowl. Combine the romaine, pears and walnuts in a salad bowl. Add the dressing and toss well. Sprinkle with the feta cheese. Yield: 4 to 6 servings.

Exotic Spinach and Strawberry Salad with Poppy Seed Dressing

2	bunches fresh spinach, torn
2	pints fresh strawberries, sliced
·	Toasted sliced almonds
1/2	cup sugar
1	tablespoon poppy seeds
2	teaspoons sesame seeds
1 1/2	teaspoons minced onion
1/4	teaspoon Worcestershire sauce
1/4	teaspoon paprika
1/4	cup cider vinegar
1/2	cup olive oil

Arrange the spinach in a salad bowl. Layer the strawberries over the spinach. Sprinkle with the toasted almonds. Combine the sugar, poppy seeds, sesame seeds, onion, Worcestershire sauce, paprika and vinegar in a blender container. Add the olive oil in a steady stream, processing constantly at low speed until creamy; do not over blend. Pour the dressing over the salad. Serve immediately. May substitute drained mandarin oranges for the strawberries. Yield: 4 to 6 servings.

Crossing the Cape Fear River at Wilmington the next morning, he ate breakfast with his friend Benjamin Smith at Belvedere Plantation and from there traveled in his carriage on what was known then as the "King's Highway." He journeyed through Conwayborough, Georgetown, and then to Charleston.

CAFÉ MAYONNAISE

5	egg yolks
2	tablespoons plus 2 teaspoons white wine vinegar
2	tablespoons Worcestershire sauce
4	teaspoons Dijon mustard
1	teaspoon Tabasco sauce
4	cups corn oil
·	Salt and white pepper to taste

Process the egg yolks, vinegar, Worcestershire sauce, mustard and Tabasco sauce in a blender at medium-high speed. Add the corn oil in a fine stream, processing constantly. Season with salt and white pepper. Yield: 4 to 4½ cups.

JALAPEÑO RANCH SALAD DRESSING

¾	bunch cilantro
1	cup buttermilk
1	cup sour cream
¼	cup chopped seeded jalapeños
1½	cloves of garlic
·	Salt and pepper to taste

Rinse the cilantro and remove the stems. Combine the buttermilk, sour cream, cilantro, jalapeños, garlic, salt and pepper in a blender container. Process until smooth. Yield: 2 cups.

BLEU CHEESE SALAD DRESSING

3/4	cup low-fat or nonfat sour cream
1	teaspoon Worcestershire sauce
1/2	teaspoon dry mustard
1/2	teaspoon salt
1/2	teaspoon pepper
1/2	teaspoon garlic powder
1 1/3	cups low-fat or nonfat mayonnaise
4	ounces Danish bleu cheese, crumbled

Combine the sour cream, Worcestershire sauce, dry mustard, salt, pepper and garlic powder in a 4-cup glass mixer bowl. Beat at low speed for 2 minutes or until blended. Add the mayonnaise. Beat at medium speed for 2 minutes. Beat at low speed for 30 seconds. Add the bleu cheese. Beat at low speed for 4 minutes. Chill, covered, for 24 hours. May also use this dressing as a dip for vegetables, chicken wings and sweet potato chips. Yield: 2 to 2 1/2 cups.

Side Dishes And Pastas

Good food and the Lower Cape Fear go hand in hand. Whether entertaining in an elegant fashion or relaxing with a casual picnic on the beach, add seasonal flair to menus with the bounty of fresh foods in season. The moderate climate along the Cape Fear Coast is one of the delightful treats of the area. A picnic is an outing that may be enjoyed on a warm November day or a day in March when the flowers begin to bloom.

ASPARAGUS WITH GARLIC AND BALSAMIC VINAIGRETTE

1/4	cup balsamic vinegar
2	shallots, chopped
2	cloves of garlic, chopped
1	teaspoon chopped fresh thyme
1/2	cup olive oil
1/4	cup vegetable oil
·	Salt and pepper to taste
1	head of garlic, roasted, skinned
1	cup sliced mushrooms
1	pound asparagus, lightly blanched, drained

Combine the balsamic vinegar, shallots, chopped garlic and thyme in a saucepan. Whisk in the olive oil and vegetable oil gradually. Season with salt and pepper. Add the roasted garlic and mushrooms. Bring to a boil. Pour over the drained asparagus in a serving bowl. Cool. Let stand at room temperature for 24 hours. Serve at room temperature. Yield: 4 servings.

MARINATED BROCCOLI

1	bunch broccoli, cut into florets
1	medium red onion, finely chopped
1/2	to 2/3 cup raisins
1/3	cup sunflower kernels
4	to 6 slices cooked bacon, crumbled
1	cup mayonnaise
1/4	to 1/3 cup vinegar
1	tablespoon sugar
·	Salt and pepper to taste

Combine the broccoli florets, onion, raisins, sunflower kernels and bacon in a large bowl. Blend the mayonnaise, vinegar, sugar, salt and pepper in a bowl. Pour over the broccoli mixture and mix well. Serve immediately. Yield: 4 to 6 servings.

Orange-Glazed Carrots

6	to 8 carrots
	Salt to taste
1/4	cup butter
1/4	cup sugar
1	tablespoon flour
·	Juice of 2 oranges (about 2/3 cup)
·	Orange slice halves

Scrape the carrots and cut into strips lengthwise. Cook in boiling salted water in a saucepan until tender; drain. Place in a shallow baking dish. Melt the butter in a small saucepan. Stir in the sugar and flour. Add the orange juice gradually, stirring constantly. Cook until thickened, stirring constantly. Pour over the carrots. Bake at 350 degrees for 30 minutes. Garnish with twisted orange slice halves. Yield: 4 to 6 servings.

Greek Green Beans

1	pound green beans, trimmed
4	scallions, chopped
1	clove of garlic, minced
1/3	cup chopped fresh mint
1/3	cup chopped fresh basil
1/3	cup chopped fresh oregano
·	Salt and pepper to taste
1/3	cup olive oil
3	tablespoons white wine vinegar
1	tablespoon lemon juice
1/2	cup crumbled feta cheese
2	hard-cooked eggs, chopped

Steam the green beans in a steamer until tender-crisp. Combine the green beans, scallions, garlic, mint, basil, oregano and salt and pepper to taste in a bowl and toss to mix well. Add a mixture of the olive oil, vinegar and lemon juice and toss to mix well. Spoon into a serving bowl. Sprinkle with the cheese and eggs. Serve hot or cold. May substitute an equivalent amount of dried herbs for fresh.
Yield: 6 servings.

By the late 1800s, the largest cotton export company in the world conducted its business from an office on Front Street, with imposing brick warehouses and wharves on Water Street. The building—appropriately named "The Cotton Exchange"—now houses specialty shops and restaurants. And in 1867 The Wilmington Morning Star was established, making it the "oldest daily newspaper in continuous publication" in the state.

LEMON GREEN BEANS

1½	pounds tender young green beans, trimmed	¼	teaspoon freshly ground pepper
½	tablespoon salt	½	teaspoon salt
2	tablespoons olive oil	3	tablespoons lemon juice
2	cloves of garlic, cut into eighths	2	tablespoons minced fresh basil, or 1 tablespoon dried

Combine the green beans and ½ tablespoon salt in water to cover in a saucepan. Cook until al dente. Pour into a colander and rinse immediately with cold water; drain. Mix the olive oil, garlic, pepper, ½ teaspoon salt, lemon juice and basil in a container with a tightfitting lid. Add the green beans. Marinate, tightly covered, at room temperature for 30 minutes, turning occasionally. May marinate the green beans in the refrigerator for 8 to 10 hours for a tangier flavor. Bring to room temperature before serving. Yield: 6 to 8 servings.

HOPPING JOHN

1	cup dried black-eyed peas	¼	teaspoon sage
12	ounces smoked ham, chopped	1	medium tomato, peeled, seeded, finely chopped
¾	cup chopped celery	3	tablespoons olive oil
¾	cup chopped onion	2	tablespoons white wine vinegar
⅓	cup chopped green bell pepper	¼	cup chopped parsley
1	clove of garlic, finely chopped	1	cup white rice
½	teaspoon thyme	·	Tabasco sauce to taste
		·	Chopped scallions

Rinse and sort the peas. Soak in water to cover in a bowl for 8 to 10 hours; drain well. Combine the peas, ham, celery, onion, green pepper, garlic, thyme and sage in a medium saucepan. Add water to cover. Bring to a boil and reduce the heat. Simmer, covered, for 35 to 40 minutes or until the peas are tender. Drain, reserving the cooking liquid. Stir the tomato into the peas. Add a mixture of the olive oil, vinegar and parsley and mix well. Combine the reserved cooking liquid with enough water in a glass measure to measure 2 cups. Pour into a saucepan and add the rice. Bring to a boil and reduce the heat to low. Cook, covered, for 18 to 20 minutes or until all the water is absorbed and the rice is tender. Add the peas. Cook until heated through. Season with Tabasco sauce. Spoon into a serving bowl. Sprinkle with chopped scallions. Yield: 6 servings.

PICKLED BLACK-EYED PEAS

3	(16-ounce) cans black-eyed peas, rinsed, drained
1/2	small green bell pepper, finely chopped (1/2 cup)
1/2	small red bell pepper, finely chopped (1/2 cup)
4	scallions with tops, thinly sliced
1/2	cup extra-virgin olive oil
1/4	cup red wine vinegar
1	clove of garlic, minced

Combine the peas, green pepper, red pepper, scallions, olive oil, vinegar and garlic in a large bowl and mix well. Chill, covered, in the refrigerator for 5 hours to 2 days. Yield: 10 servings.

ELEGANT GREEN PEAS

4	slices bacon, cut into strips
1/2	large onion, chopped
1	cup fresh mushrooms
1	tablespoon flour
1	cup whipping cream
·	Salt and freshly ground pepper to taste
1/4	cup sherry
1	(20-ounce) can green peas, drained

Sauté the bacon, onion and mushrooms in a large skillet until the bacon is brown. Add the flour, whipping cream, salt and pepper, stirring constantly. Cook over low heat until thickened, stirring constantly. Add the sherry. Fold in the peas. Cook until heated through. May use canned mushrooms instead of the fresh mushrooms and add to the sauce with the sherry. Yield: 4 servings.

SUGAR SNAP PEAS IN TOASTED SESAME VINAIGRETTE

1	pound fresh sugar snap peas
1/4	cup sesame seeds
1	small clove of garlic, crushed
1	teaspoon Dijon mustard
1	tablespoon fresh lemon juice
1/4	teaspoon salt
1/4	teaspoon pepper
1	tablespoon red wine vinegar
1/4	cup olive oil
3/4	teaspoon Oriental sesame oil

Cook the peas in boiling water in a large saucepan for 30 seconds or until tender-crisp. Drain and rinse under cold water. Toast the sesame seeds in a skillet over medium heat for 3 minutes or until brown. Pour onto a plate and let stand until cool. Combine the garlic, mustard, lemon juice, salt and pepper in a medium bowl. Stir in the vinegar. Whisk in the olive oil and sesame oil. Add the peas and toasted sesame seeds and toss to mix well. Serve at room temperature or chilled. May use frozen sugar snap peas instead of the fresh, but do not blanch. Let the peas thaw on paper towels and come to room temperature before using. This recipe is also good with julienned yellow squash and zucchini. Yield: 4 to 6 servings.

SUNDAY POTATOES

5	pounds potatoes, peeled, chopped
1/2	cup butter
8	ounces cream cheese, softened
2	cups sour cream
1/3	jar chives
·	Paprika to taste

Boil the potatoes in water to cover in a saucepan until tender; drain. Add the butter and cream cheese. Beat until smooth. Beat in the sour cream and chives. Pour into a 2-quart baking dish. Sprinkle with paprika. Bake at 375 degrees for 30 minutes. Yield: 6 to 8 servings.

BOURBON SWEET POTATOES

4	to 5 medium sweet potatoes, peeled, chopped
1/2	teaspoon salt
1/2	cup butter
3	eggs
1	(8-ounce) can crushed pineapple
1/2	cup evaporated milk
1	cup packed brown sugar
2	tablespoons bourbon
6	tablespoons melted butter
2	cups Grape-Nuts flakes
1/2	cup pecan halves
1	tablespoon brown sugar

Combine the sweet potatoes, salt and water to cover in a saucepan. Simmer for 40 minutes or until tender; drain. Combine the sweet potatoes, 1/2 cup butter and eggs in a bowl and beat until smooth. Add the pineapple, evaporated milk, 1 cup brown sugar and bourbon and mix well. Spoon into a large baking dish. Mix the 6 tablespoons butter, Grape-Nuts flakes and pecan halves in a bowl. Sprinkle over the sweet potato mixture. Sprinkle with 1 tablespoon brown sugar. Bake at 325 degrees for 15 minutes. Yield: 4 to 6 servings.

LAYERED SQUASH CASSEROLE

2	each medium yellow squash and zucchini, thinly sliced
1	medium onion, thinly sliced
1	cup thinly sliced fresh mushrooms
1/2	teaspoon salt
1/4	teaspoon ground pepper
·	Chopped fresh thyme to taste
1	medium tomato, sliced
2	tablespoons butter
2	tablespoons freshly grated Parmesan cheese

Layer the squash, zucchini, onion and mushrooms in an 8x8-inch baking dish, sprinkling each layer with salt, pepper and thyme. Arrange the tomato slices over the layers and dot with the butter. Sprinkle with the cheese. Bake at 350 degrees for 35 minutes or until tender-crisp. May double the recipe and bake in a 9x13-inch baking dish. Yield: 6 servings.

SQUASH FRITTERS

A simple, old-fashioned recipe that is good when fresh squash are plentiful in the garden.

1¼	cups self-rising flour
¾	teaspoon salt
½	teaspoon sugar
½	cup sour cream
1	egg, lightly beaten
1	tablespoon vegetable oil
1	medium onion, grated
3	cups grated yellow squash or zucchini
¼	cup vegetable oil

Sift the flour, salt and sugar into a bowl. Add the sour cream, egg and 1 tablespoon vegetable oil and mix lightly. Fold in the onion and squash. Heat some of the remaining vegetable oil in a skillet. Drop the batter by tablespoonfuls into the hot skillet. Fry until golden brown on both sides, turning once. Repeat with the remaining batter and vegetable oil. Yield: 4 to 6 servings.

SUMMER TOMATOES WITH ASIAN DRESSING

The Asian Dressing is excellent on green salads when fresh summer tomatoes aren't available.

4	tomatoes, sliced
1	pound mozzarella cheese, cut into 1/2-inch pieces
2	teaspoons soy sauce
2	teaspoons water
1	green onion, chopped
·	Juice of 1 lemon
1/2	teaspoon sesame oil
1/4	teaspoon hot pepper chile oil
1	clove of garlic, finely chopped
1/4	teaspoon pepper
·	Salt to taste
3/4	cup peanut oil
7	teaspoons rice wine vinegar

Alternate layers of the tomatoes and cheese in a serving bowl. Combine the soy sauce, water, green onion, lemon juice, sesame oil, hot pepper chile oil, garlic, pepper and salt in a jar with a tightfitting lid. Cover and shake until well blended. Add the peanut oil. Cover and shake again. Let stand for 3 minutes. Add the vinegar. Cover and shake well. Pour over the layers. Serve immediately.
Yield: 4 to 6 servings.

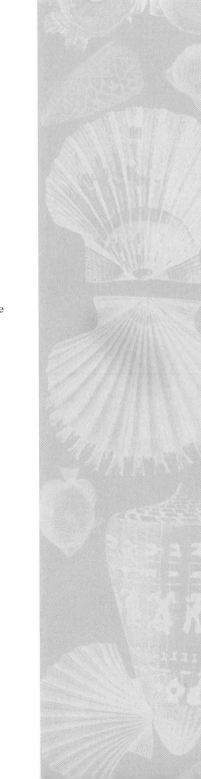

FRIED GREEN TOMATOES

¾	cup self-rising flour
¾	cup cornmeal mix
1	large egg
⅓	cup buttermilk
½	cup vegetable oil
2	large green tomatoes, sliced ¼ inch thick
·	Salt to taste

Mix the flour and cornmeal mix in a shallow pan. Mix the egg and buttermilk in a bowl. Heat the oil in a 10- or 12-inch skillet over medium heat. Dip the tomato slices in the egg mixture and then roll in the flour mixture. Place in a single layer in the preheated skillet. Fry until golden brown on both sides, turning once. Remove to a plate lined with 4 paper towels to drain. Sprinkle with salt. Repeat with the remaining tomato slices. Yield: 6 servings.

SAFFRON RICE-STUFFED TOMATOES

1	(5-ounce) package saffron rice
1	onion, finely chopped
1	tablespoon extra-virgin olive oil
4	large tomatoes
1	teaspoon dillweed
½	cup grated Parmesan cheese
4	pats of butter

Prepare the rice using the package directions. Sauté the onion in the olive oil in a medium skillet over medium heat. Core the tomatoes. Remove the pulp from the tomatoes into a bowl and set the tomato shells aside. Chop the tomato pulp. Add the rice, onion and dillweed and mix well. Spoon into the tomato shells. Place in a glass baking dish sprayed with nonstick cooking spray. Top each tomato with 2 tablespoons Parmesan cheese and a pat of butter. Bake at 350 degrees for 15 to 20 minutes or until the cheese is lightly browned. Remove from the oven. Let the tomatoes stand for 5 minutes before serving. Yield: 4 servings.

Zucchini Casserole

2   pounds zucchini, sliced
·   Salt to taste
1½   cups thinly sliced celery
1   cup finely chopped onion
2   tablespoons butter
3   eggs, lightly beaten
½   cup whipping cream
2   tablespoons melted butter
1   teaspoon salt
½   teaspoon white pepper
1½   cups shredded Cheddar cheese
9   slices cooked bacon, crumbled

Cook the zucchini in boiling salted water in a saucepan until tender; drain and mash. Sauté the celery and onion in 2 tablespoons butter in a skillet until transparent. Combine the zucchini, eggs, whipping cream and 2 tablespoons melted butter in a bowl and mix well. Add the sautéed vegetables, salt, white pepper and ¾ cup of the cheese and mix well. Pour into a nonstick 9x13-inch baking dish. Sprinkle with the remaining cheese and bacon. Bake at 350 degrees for 45 minutes. Serve immediately. Yield: 8 to 10 servings.

Zucchini and Tomato Gratin

3   medium zucchini, thinly sliced
4   medium tomatoes, peeled, thinly sliced
¾   cup grated Parmesan cheese
2   cloves of garlic, minced
1   teaspoon thyme
¼   teaspoon salt
¼   teaspoon pepper
2   tablespoons olive oil

Layer ½ of the zucchini and ½ of the tomatoes in a greased 8x8-inch baking dish. Sprinkle with ¼ cup of the Parmesan cheese. Layer the remaining zucchini and tomatoes over the Parmesan cheese. Sprinkle with the garlic, thyme, salt and pepper. Drizzle with the olive oil. Sprinkle with the remaining Parmesan cheese. Bake at 400 degrees for 20 to 25 minutes or until bubbly.
Yield: 4 to 6 servings.

BROWN AND WILD RICE DRESSING

1½	cups brown rice
½	cup wild rice
4	cups chicken broth
1	tablespoon butter
·	Salt to taste
½	cup sliced almonds
⅓	cup butter
1	cup sliced fresh mushrooms
2	ribs celery, sliced
2	to 3 green onions, coarsely chopped
½	teaspoon fresh thyme, or ¼ teaspoon dried
¼	cup chopped fresh parsley

Combine the brown rice and wild rice in a strainer. Rinse with cold water until the water runs clear. Bring the broth, 1 tablespoon butter and salt to a boil in a saucepan. Stir the rice into the boiling broth. Reduce the heat to low. Cook, covered, for 45 to 50 minutes; do not uncover. Remove from the heat. Let stand for 10 to 15 minutes. Sauté the almonds in ⅓ cup butter in a skillet. Add the mushrooms and celery. Sauté until the celery is tender-crisp. Add to the cooked rice and toss to mix well. Add the green onions, thyme and parsley and toss to mix well. Spoon into a serving bowl and serve immediately. Yield: 8 to 10 servings.

SAUSAGE DRESSING

This recipe won in a city-wide contest.

1	pound hot sausage
2	medium onions, chopped
5	to 6 ribs celery, chopped
1	long loaf thinly sliced white bread, toasted
3/4	(16-ounce) package Pepperidge Farm dressing
1	teaspoon sage
1/2	teaspoon salt
1/2	teaspoon pepper

Crumble the sausage into a skillet. Add the onions. Cook until the sausage is brown, stirring constantly. Do not drain. Bring the celery and enough water to cover to a boil in a saucepan. Cook until the celery is tender. Drain, reserving the cooking liquid. Tear the bread into small pieces into an extra-large bowl. Add the dressing and toss to mix well. Stir in the undrained sausage mixture. Add the sage, salt and pepper and mix well. Stir in the celery. Add just enough of the reserved hot liquid gradually to moisten the dry ingredients, stirring constantly. Spoon into a nonstick 9x13-inch baking dish. Bake at 350 degrees for 30 minutes or until the top is golden brown. May store, tightly wrapped, in the freezer.
Yield: 20 servings.

Chartered in 1852, Oakdale Cemetery nestles among oak trees in the Mansion District. It is the final resting place of many notable people: war heroes, unknown soldiers, a spy, governors, politicians, an unfortunate dueler, and even a young girl entombed in a cask of rum. Especially intriguing is the story of William A. Ellerbrook, a riverboat captain who lost his life in 1880 fighting a fire at Front and Dock streets. His faithful dog "Boss" died alongside him while trying to save his master's life and was buried in the same casket. The monument depicts a dog in bas-relief with the words, "Faithful Unto Death."

OYSTERS JOHNNY REB

Reliable and good, this southern Thanksgiving favorite is one that most people like spicy.

2	quarts oysters, drained
1/2	cup finely chopped parsley
1/2	cup finely chopped shallot or onion
1/2	clove of garlic, pressed
3	tablespoons chopped green bell pepper
·	Salt and pepper to taste
·	Tabasco sauce to taste
1	tablespoon Worcestershire sauce
2	tablespoons lemon juice
1/2	cup (or less) melted margarine
2	cups (or less) fine cracker crumbs
·	Paprika to taste
3/4	cup half-and-half

Layer the oysters, parsley, shallot, garlic, green pepper, salt, pepper, Tabasco sauce, Worcestershire sauce, lemon juice, margarine and cracker crumbs 1/2 at a time in a greased 2-quart baking dish. Sprinkle with paprika. Make evenly spaced holes in the top. Pour the half-and-half into the holes, being careful not to moisten the crumb topping all over. Bake at 375 degrees for 30 minutes. Yield: 12 to 15 servings.

In the 1860s, conductor Joe Baldwin frantically signaled an oncoming train that was on a collision course with his uncoupled car. Joe's efforts could not prevent the crash; he lost his life and his head. For the next ninety years, thousands would come to Maco Station, fourteen miles west of Wilmington, to see a light come up out of the swamp and swing down the tracks—it was said to be the spirit of Joe Baldwin looking for his head.

➤

SMOKED CHEESE GRITS

4	cups water
1	tablespoon salt
1	teaspoon freshly ground pepper
1	cup stone-ground white grits
1/2	cup stone-ground yellow grits
3/4	cup grated smoked Gouda cheese
1/4	cup whipping cream
1/4	cup butter
1	teaspoon Tabasco sauce

Bring the water, salt and pepper to a boil in a large saucepan. Add the white and yellow grits gradually, whisking constantly until smooth. Cook for 15 to 20 minutes or until thickened, stirring occasionally. Fold in the cheese, whipping cream and butter. Stir in the Tabasco sauce. Adjust the seasonings. Serve immediately. Yield: 6 to 8 servings.

COUSCOUS WITH FRESH VEGETABLES

1	(6-ounce) package couscous
1	cup chopped broccoli
1	cup shredded carrots
1	cup chopped red potatoes
1	cup chopped yellow squash
3/4	cup olive oil
1/2	cup lemon juice
2	cloves of garlic, minced
1	teaspoon Dijon mustard
1	teaspoon coriander
1	teaspoon salt
·	Pepper to taste

Prepare the couscous using the package directions. Sauté the broccoli, carrots, potatoes and squash in the olive oil in a large skillet until tender. Mix the lemon juice, garlic, mustard, coriander, salt and pepper in a small bowl. Combine the sautéed vegetables, couscous and lemon juice mixture in a medium bowl and mix well. Spoon into a serving bowl and serve immediately. Yield: 6 servings.

Following a visit from President Grover Cleveland in 1889, the mysterious Maco light was researched by the Smithsonian, shot at by the Army, and written about in Life Magazine. After the tracks were taken up in 1977, sightings stopped. Hopefully the spirit of Joe Baldwin is finally at rest.

TABOULI

1	(1-pound) package bulgur
2	pounds 6½ ounces tomatoes
10	ounces green onions, finely chopped
6	ounces white onions, finely chopped
2½	tablespoons salt
1	teaspoon pepper
5	bunches parsley, finely chopped
2	bunches mint, finely chopped
¾	cup plus 1 tablespoon olive oil (6½ ounces)
7	tablespoons lemon juice (3½ ounces)
·	Tender grape, lettuce or cabbage leaves

Prepare and cook the bulgur using the package directions. Peel and chop the tomatoes into small pieces. Combine the green onions and white onions in a large bowl. Sprinkle with the salt and pepper. Add the bulgur, tomatoes, parsley and mint and mix well. Add the olive oil and lemon juice gradually, mixing well after each addition. Spoon onto a large serving platter. Serve with grape, lettuce or cabbage leaves or a combination of the three. Yield: 8 to 10 servings.

RISOTTO WITH GREEN PEAS AND PANCETTA

4	cups chicken broth
1/4	cup chopped pancetta
1	onion, finely chopped
1	cup arborio rice
1	cup fresh green peas
·	Salt and freshly ground white pepper to taste
1	cup grated Parmesan cheese

Heat the chicken broth in a saucepan. Sauté the pancetta in a nonstick
2-quart saucepan over medium-high heat until crisp and golden brown. Add the
onion. Sauté for 3 minutes or until transparent. Stir in the rice. Cook for 1 to
2 minutes or until the rice is evenly coated. Add the heated chicken broth 1 cup
at a time, cooking after each addition for 5 to 6 minutes or until all of the broth has
been absorbed and stirring constantly. Stir in the green peas. Cook for 2 minutes or
until the green peas are heated through. Season with salt and white pepper. Sprinkle
with the Parmesan cheese and white pepper. Yield: 10 servings.

HERBED BOW TIE AND STEAK SALAD

1	(12-ounce) New York strip steak, trimmed
·	Soy sauce
1/2	cup fresh lemon juice
1/4	cup virgin olive oil
1	clove of garlic, crushed (optional)
2	tablespoons olive oil
1	pound bow ties
·	Salt to taste
1	teaspoon ground cumin
1/4	cup chopped fresh Italian flat-leaf parsley
1/2	to 1 cup chopped fresh cilantro leaves (optional)
1/2	cup chopped fresh basil
1/4	cup chopped fresh mint leaves (optional)
1/4	to 1 cup torn fresh arugula
1	red bell pepper, thinly sliced (optional)
·	Fresh lemon juice or grated fresh Parmesan or Romano cheese to taste (optional)

Marinate the steak in soy sauce to cover in a container in the refrigerator. Combine the 1/2 cup lemon juice, 1/4 cup olive oil and garlic in a bowl and mix well. Let stand at room temperature. Heat 2 tablespoons olive oil in a skillet. Drain the steak and add to the skillet. Sear on both sides and reduce the heat. Cook until of the desired degree of doneness and remove from the heat and keep warm. Cook the pasta in boiling salted water in a saucepan until al dente. Remove and discard the garlic from the olive oil mixture. Add the cumin, parsley, cilantro, basil and mint and mix well. Add the arugula and red pepper. Drain the pasta and place in an extra-large bowl. Add the herb mixture and mix well. Cut the steak into thin slices. Add to the pasta mixture and toss to mix well. Sprinkle with lemon juice to taste.
Yield: 4 to 6 servings.

CHICKEN AND PASTA SALAD

1	cup vegetable oil
1/2	cup sugar
1/3	cup catsup
1/4	cup vinegar
2	tablespoons Worcestershire sauce
1	(1 1/2- to 2-pound) package boneless chicken breasts
·	Ground ginger to taste
·	Garlic salt to taste
·	Olive oil
·	Soy sauce to taste
8	ounces rainbow rotini
1/2	bunch broccoli, cut into florets
4	green onions with tops, chopped
1	green or red bell pepper, cut into thin strips
1/2	(10-ounce) package pea pods, thawed

Combine the vegetable oil, sugar, catsup, vinegar and Worcestershire sauce in a bowl and mix well. Pour into a cruet. Chill in the refrigerator. Sprinkle the chicken with ginger and garlic salt. Sear the chicken in a small amount of hot olive oil in a skillet. Add soy sauce. Cook over medium-high heat until the chicken is brown and reduce the heat. Cook, covered, until tender and cooked through, adding more soy sauce as needed. Cook the pasta using the package directions; drain. Cut the chicken into bite-size pieces. Combine the pasta, chicken, broccoli, green onions, green pepper and pea pods in a large bowl and toss to mix well. Add 1/2 of the dressing and toss to mix well. Chill, covered, in the refrigerator. Store the remaining dressing in the refrigerator for another purpose for up to several weeks. Yield: 6 to 8 servings.

Goods included teas, silks, perfumes, and French fashions. The profits were not without risk: during the first nine days of February 1864, six blockade runners wrecked off Cape Fear. Due to dramatic high-speed chases and the shoal-infested waters of Cape Fear, more than thirty blockade runners were counted as total losses.

COLD CHICKEN AND PASTA PLATTER

Since the flavor of this recipe is enhanced by preparing the day before, it is a great dish to take to someone's house or on a picnic.

1	pound vermicelli
4	skinless boneless chicken breasts
½	cup olive oil
2	tablespoons butter
2	(6-ounce) jars marinated artichoke hearts
1	to 2 tablespoons rice wine vinegar
1	tablespoon (rounded) mayonnaise
5	scallions, chopped
4	cloves of garlic, minced
¼	to ½ cup chopped fresh tarragon leaves
·	Salt to taste

Cook the pasta al dente using the package directions; drain. Cut the chicken into bite-size pieces. Heat the olive oil and butter in a skillet. Add the chicken. Cook until the chicken is cooked through and remove from the heat. Drain the artichoke hearts, reserving the marinade. Cut the artichoke hearts into quarters. Whisk the vinegar and mayonnaise in a large bowl. Add the scallions and garlic and mix well. Add the artichoke hearts, reserved marinade, undrained chicken, pasta, tarragon and salt, tossing to mix well after each addition. Chill, covered, in the refrigerator for 8 to 10 hours. Spoon onto a large platter to serve. Yield: 6 to 8 servings.

Note: Tarragon has a more pungent flavor as it blends with the olive oil. Begin this recipe by using a small amount of tarragon and adjust the amount according to your taste. Dried tarragon may be used (⅓ teaspoon ground or 1½ teaspoons crushed dried tarragon is equivalent to 1 tablespoon of the fresh).

CHICKEN WITH LEMON CAPER CREAM

1/4	cup butter
1	medium onion, chopped
1	pound boneless skinless chicken breasts, cut into strips
1/4	to 1/2 cup lemon juice
2	cups cream
1/4	cup drained capers
1	pound pasta, cooked
1/4	cup chopped fresh parsley

Melt the butter in a large skillet over medium heat. Add the onion. Sauté for 1 minute. Increase the heat to medium-high. Add the chicken. Sauté until light brown. Add the lemon juice, stirring with a wooden spoon to deglaze the skillet. Cook until most of the lemon juice has evaporated. Stir in the cream. Simmer for 10 to 12 minutes or until thickened, stirring constantly. Stir in the capers. Serve immediately over hot cooked pasta. Sprinkle with the parsley. Yield: 6 servings.

In 1863 she boarded the blockade runner Ad-Vance out of Wilmington that bravely steamed through the Union fleet and arrived safely in England. There her artist son, James McNeill Abbott Whistler, painted her quiet countenance. This painting can be seen today in the Louvre in Paris and is known to millions as "Whistler's Mother."

CHICKEN MARSALA

4	boneless skinless chicken breasts
1/2	cup flour
2	tablespoons olive oil
1	teaspoon butter
·	Juice of 1 lemon
1	cup marsala
2	red onions, sliced
1	green bell pepper, cut into strips
1	red bell pepper, cut into strips
1	pound sliced fresh mushrooms
1/4	cup olive oil
8	ounces vermicelli
8	ounces angel hair pasta
·	Freshly squeezed lemon juice to taste
·	Olive oil to taste
·	Chopped fresh parsley to taste
·	Salt to taste
·	Freshly cracked black peppercorns

Wrap each chicken breast in waxed paper or plastic wrap. Pound each side with a meat mallet until thin. Dredge the chicken lightly in the flour. Heat 2 tablespoons olive oil and the butter in a skillet. Add the chicken. Cook for 2 to 3 minutes per side or until brown. Squeeze the juice of 1 lemon over the chicken. Cook until the lemon juice is reduced. Add the wine. Cook until the wine is reduced. Sauté the onions, green pepper, red pepper and mushrooms in 1/4 cup olive oil in a skillet. Cook, covered, for 20 minutes. Cook, uncovered, for 10 minutes longer or until the vegetables are caramelized. Cook the pastas using package directions and drain. Add freshly squeezed lemon juice to taste, olive oil to taste and parsley to taste and toss to mix well. Spoon the vegetables onto 4 dinner plates. Arrange the chicken over the vegetables. Arrange the pasta by the side of the chicken. Sprinkle with salt, pepper and fresh parsley to taste. Yield: 4 servings.

PASTA WITH COUNTRY HAM, SNOW PEAS AND ASPARAGUS

1½	pounds fresh asparagus, trimmed
8	ounces snow peas
6	ounces country ham, julienned
1	tablespoon butter
1	cup whipping cream
16	ounces bow tie pasta
3	ounces Parmesan cheese, freshly grated
2	tablespoons minced fresh parsley
1½	teaspoons tarragon
2	ounces pine nuts, toasted
·	Steamed mussels

Cook the asparagus in water to cover in a saucepan for 2 to 3 minutes or until tender-crisp. Drain and rinse under cold water. Snap off the tips. Cut the stalks into ¾-inch pieces. String the snow peas. Cook in boiling water to cover for 30 to 60 seconds or until tender-crisp. Drain and rinse under cold water. Cut into diagonal pieces. Sauté the ham in the butter over medium-low heat for 2 to 3 minutes. Add the whipping cream. Cook over medium-high heat for a few minutes or until thickened, stirring constantly. Cook the pasta until al dente using package directions; drain. Place on a large serving platter. Add the asparagus tips and pieces, snow peas, sautéed ham mixture, Parmesan cheese, parsley and tarragon and toss to mix well. Garnish with pine nuts and steamed mussels. Serve immediately with additional freshly grated Parmesan cheese. Yield: 6 to 8 servings.

Wilmington was plagued by two
devastating recurring problems:
fire and yellow fever. The
blockade runner Kate from
Nassau brought a most
unwelcome visitor to Wilmington
in June 1862—yellow fever, or
"General Yellow Jack." Having
suffered an earlier yellow fever
epidemic in 1821, those who
could leave fled the town and
businesses closed. Those who
stayed behind to care for
the sick paid a heavy price.
Three ministers, two doctors,
three druggists, and over six
hundred fifty people died.

►

BOW TIES WITH SAUSAGE AND PEPPERS

12	ounces sweet or hot Italian sausage, cut into ¹/2-inch pieces
1	medium onion, chopped (¹/2 cup)
2	cloves of garlic, minced
1	large red bell pepper, cut into 1-inch pieces
1	large green bell pepper, cut into 1-inch pieces
1	cup sliced fresh mushrooms
²/3	cup chicken broth
1	tablespoon chopped fresh basil, or 1 teaspoon crushed dried basil
2	teaspoons cornstarch
1	large tomato, coarsely chopped (1 cup)
6	ounces bow ties, cooked, drained

Cook the sausage, onion and garlic in a large skillet for 5 minutes. Add the red pepper, green pepper and mushrooms. Cook for 5 minutes or until the sausage is brown; drain. Combine the broth, basil and cornstarch in a small bowl. Add to the sausage mixture. Cook until thickened and bubbly, stirring constantly. Cook for 2 minutes longer, stirring constantly. Stir in the tomato. Cook until heated through. Pour over the hot cooked pasta in a serving bowl and toss to mix well.
Yield: 4 servings.

RIGATONI WITH SCALLOPS

2   cups dry white wine

1   tablespoon grated lemon peel

1   pound bay scallops

4   teaspoons Dijon mustard

4   tablespoons butter

12   ounces rigatoni, cooked, drained

·   Salt and pepper to taste

1   tablespoon chopped chives or parsley

Bring the wine and lemon peel to a simmer in a large skillet. Add the scallops. Cook for 1 minute or until tender. Remove the scallops from the skillet using a slotted spoon and set aside to keep warm. Increase the heat and bring the pan drippings to a boil. Boil for 5 minutes or until the liquid is reduced by half. Whisk in the mustard. Add the butter 1 tablespoon at a time, whisking constantly after each addition. Add the pasta, scallops, salt and pepper and toss to mix well. Place in a serving bowl. Sprinkle with the chives. Yield: 4 servings.

General Yellow Jack held the town captive for five terrible months until a November frost stopped its spread. Help poured into Wilmington from other towns and states. Wilmingtonians reciprocated the kindness sixty-five years later in 1886, when Charleston, South Carolina, suffered its devastating earthquake.

SHRIMP ELEGANTE

3	pounds fresh large shrimp
·	Salt to taste
1/2	cup butter or margarine
3/4	cup olive oil
2	cups coarsely chopped onions
3	cloves of garlic, crushed
1/4	cup chopped fresh parsley
1	teaspoon dried oregano
1/2	cup dry white wine
1/3	cup Italian salad dressing
1/4	cup water
4	teaspoons instant chicken bouillon
·	Freshly ground pepper to taste
8	ounces fettuccini

Peel the shrimp leaving the tails intact. Devein and butterfly the shrimp. Cook in boiling salted water in a saucepan for 30 seconds. Drain and place in a shallow broiling pan. Melt the butter with the olive oil in a large saucepan over medium heat. Add the onions, garlic, parsley and oregano. Cook until the onions are transparent, stirring constantly. Stir in the wine, salad dressing, water, instant bouillon and pepper. Reduce the heat to low. Cook for 5 minutes. Pour over the shrimp. Chill, covered, for 2 hours to overnight. Cook the fettuccini using package directions and drain. Uncover the shrimp. Broil 4 inches from the heat source for 5 minutes on each side or until the shrimp turn pink. Serve over the hot fettuccini. Yield: 6 servings.

ARTICHOKE AND CAPER PASTA

2	tablespoons butter
2	tablespoons olive oil
2	medium onions, chopped
2	cloves of garlic, crushed
3	tablespoons flour
1	cup chicken stock
3/4	cup dry white wine
1	(16-ounce) can Italian tomatoes, drained
1	(14-ounce) can artichoke hearts, drained, chopped
2	teaspoons dried basil
2	tablespoons drained capers
•	Salt and pepper to taste
•	Fusilli or tagliatelle, cooked
•	Freshly grated Parmesan cheese

Melt the butter with olive oil in a skillet. Add the onions and garlic. Sauté until the onions are pale golden brown. Stir in the flour. Add the chicken stock and wine. Cook until thickened, stirring constantly. Add the tomatoes, artichoke hearts, basil, capers, salt and pepper. Reduce the heat. Simmer for 5 to 7 minutes to enhance the flavors. Serve over hot cooked pasta. Sprinkle with Parmesan cheese. Yield: 4 to 6 servings.

Maffitt then ordered, "Full speed ahead!", thwarting Yankee efforts to seize both him and his cargo. Once the Federals realized he was getting away, fierce shelling ensued. Captain Maffitt and his cargo of ninety thousand pounds of gunpowder arrived in Wilmington in spring 1862 miraculously intact.

FETTUCCINI WITH ASPARAGUS

Serve this good summer side dish with grilled chicken.

1	pound thin asparagus, trimmed
12	ounces fettuccini
2	tablespoons unsalted butter
1	cup whipping cream
2	tablespoons extra-virgin olive oil
·	Juice of 1 lemon
·	Salt and pepper to taste
·	Zest of 1 lemon
·	Grated Parmesan cheese

Blanch the asparagus in a blanching pan for 2 minutes or until tender-crisp. Remove the colander of asparagus and plunge into a bowl of ice water, reserving the asparagus cooking liquid. Add enough water to the reserved cooking liquid to cook the fettuccini and bring to a boil. Add the fettuccini. Cook until al dente and drain. Drain the asparagus and cut into 2-inch pieces. Melt the butter in a saucepan over medium heat. Add the whipping cream and bring just to a simmer, stirring frequently. Sauté the asparagus in the olive oil in a large sauté pan. Stir in the cream mixture and lemon juice. Season with salt and pepper. Cook for a few minutes or until the flavors blend. Pour over the fettuccini in a large serving bowl and toss to mix well. Sprinkle with lemon zest and Parmesan cheese and toss lightly.
Yield: 4 servings.

CHAMPAGNE PASTA

1	(8-ounce) package frozen chopped spinach
4	cloves of garlic, minced
2	tablespoons virgin olive oil
1	pound sliced mushrooms
2	cups Champagne
1	(10-ounce) can cream of chicken soup
1	cup raisins
1	teaspoon pumpkin pie spice
1	pound penne, cooked
·	Shredded Romano cheese
·	Freshly ground pepper

Microwave the spinach in the package for 5 minutes or until defrosted. Remove from the package and drain well. Brown the garlic in olive oil in a 14-inch skillet. Add the mushrooms and 1 cup of the Champagne. Simmer, covered, for 10 minutes, stirring frequently. Stir in the spinach. Cook, uncovered, over medium heat for 5 minutes, stirring frequently. Add the soup, raisins, pumpkin pie spice and remaining Champagne. Cook until the sauce is of the desired consistency, stirring frequently. Pour over the hot pasta in a serving bowl. Sprinkle with Romano cheese and pepper. Yield: 4 servings.

Eluding Union vessels, the Condor crashed on a sandbar in New Inlet on September 30, and Rose drowned in the breakers. Hundreds gathered to pay their respects to the only woman to die in official service to the Confederacy; she was buried in Oakdale Cemetery with full military honors.

Main Dishes

If the lack of space or furniture keeps you from entertaining, host a buffet supper—one of Benjamin Franklin's inventions. When he was Ambassador to France, Franklin was asked to host a party celebrating the Fourth of July. He lacked equipment, space, and confidence to compete with the lavish Parisians. He had all the food placed on a long table; they would eat standing up. Having invited more people than the house would hold, the guests were overflowing into the garden. Ben Franklin called his party a buffet supper. The buffet became the rage in Paris and all of France—so much so that the French designed a piece of furniture called the buffet, where the diner serves himself.

LONDON BROIL

Good company and a warm climate make grilling in the South an event.

1	cup vegetable oil
¾	cup soy sauce
½	cup lemon juice
¼	cup prepared mustard
¼	cup Worcestershire sauce
¼	cup chopped onion
1	teaspoon minced garlic
1	to 2 teaspoons freshly cracked black peppercorns
1	(1½- to 2-pound) London broil

Combine the vegetable oil, soy sauce, lemon juice, mustard and Worcestershire sauce in a bowl and mix well. Stir in the onion, garlic and peppercorns. Place the London broil in a shallow glass dish. Add the marinade. Marinate, covered, in the refrigerator for 8 to 10 hours. Place the London broil on a preheated grill rack. Grill for 7 minutes on each side or until done to taste.
Yield: 2 to 4 servings.

GRILLED BEEF TENDERLOIN DIABLO

1½   cups dry sherry

1½   cups sesame oil

½   cup orange juice or pineapple juice

1   small onion, minced

3   cloves of garlic, pressed

2   tablespoons chopped green onions

1   tablespoon chopped basil

1   tablespoon chopped chives

1   tablespoon chopped oregano

1   teaspoon salt

1   teaspoon ground pepper

1½   teaspoons Tabasco sauce

·   Worcestershire sauce to taste

·   Soy sauce to taste

2   bay leaves

1   whole beef tenderloin, trimmed

·   Kosher salt

Combine the sherry, sesame oil, orange juice, onion, garlic, green onions, basil, chives, oregano, salt, pepper, Tabasco sauce, Worcestershire sauce, soy sauce and bay leaves in a glass dish and mix well. Add the beef. Marinate, covered, in the refrigerator for 24 to 48 hours, turning every 6 hours. Remove the beef from the marinade and roll in kosher salt until all sides are coated. Let stand for a few minutes. Roll in the kosher salt again. Place the beef on a preheated grill rack. Grill for 30 minutes or to the desired degree of doneness, turning frequently. Serve warm or cold. Yield: 10 servings.

Note: Some of the kosher salt will fall off during grilling and slicing. The kosher salt coating diluted by the juices is quite good and may be eaten with the beef.

Wilmington surrendered February 22. With the capture of Fort Fisher and the end of blockade running, General Robert E. Lee surrendered his sword at Appomattox on April 9, 1865. After four years of battle, war-weary soldiers slowly returned home. Reconstruction officially began on February 20, 1866, when Wilmington became a city again by charter from the North Carolina General Assembly.

SWEET-AND-SOUR LAMB SHANKS

1	cup honey
1/2	cup lemon juice
1/2	teaspoon salt
2	bay leaves
6	whole black peppercorns
1	cup boiling water
6	lamb shanks
6	small red potatoes, halved
16	pitted prunes
1/4	cup chopped fresh parsley

Combine the honey, lemon juice, salt, bay leaves, peppercorns and boiling water in a bowl and mix well. Place the lamb in a 4-quart Dutch oven. Pour the honey mixture over the lamb. Bake, covered, at 450 degrees for 1 1/2 hours. Reduce the oven temperature to 350 degrees. Add the potatoes and prunes. Bake, uncovered, for 1 hour or until tender, basting occasionally. Discard the bay leaves. Remove the lamb, prunes and potatoes to a serving platter. Sprinkle with the parsley. Yield: 6 servings.

Rio Grande Pork Roast

This is not only good, it is delicious.

1	(4- to 5-pound) boneless rolled pork loin roast
1/2	teaspoon salt
1/2	teaspoon garlic salt
1	teaspoon chili powder
1/2	cup apple jelly
1/2	cup catsup
1	tablespoon vinegar
1	cup crushed corn chips

Place the pork fat side up on a rack in a shallow roasting pan. Combine the salt, garlic salt and 1/2 teaspoon of the chili powder in a small bowl and mix well. Rub the seasoning mixture into the pork. Bake at 325 degrees for 2 to 2 1/2 hours or to 165 degrees on a meat thermometer. Combine the jelly, catsup, vinegar and the remaining 1/2 teaspoon chili powder in a small saucepan. Bring to a boil and reduce the heat. Simmer for 2 minutes. Brush the pork with the glaze. Sprinkle with the corn chips. Bake for 10 to 15 minutes or to 170 degrees on a meat thermometer. Remove the pork to a serving platter. Let stand for 10 minutes before serving. Yield: 12 servings.

SOUR CREAM PORK CHOPS

4	thick pork chops
2	tablespoons vegetable oil
1	small to medium onion, sliced
2	cups beef bouillon
1	(8-ounce) jar sliced mushrooms, drained
2	teaspoons prepared mustard
2	tablespoons chopped parsley
·	Salt and pepper to taste
1	cup sour cream

Brown the pork chops in the vegetable oil in a large skillet over medium heat; drain. Separate the onion slices into rings and arrange over the pork chops. Mix the bouillon, mushrooms, mustard, parsley, salt and pepper in a bowl. Pour over the onions. Simmer for 1 hour or until the pork chops are cooked through. Stir in the sour cream. Cook for 15 minutes. Serve with hot cooked rice or pasta. May use light sour cream. Yield: 4 servings.

President Woodrow Wilson was a citizen of Wilmington while his father was minister of First Presbyterian Church. Known as "Tommy" Wilson, he's remembered as a youth for having the town's first high-wheel bicycle, which unfortunately he rode into the Cape Fear River one day while trying to navigate the steep decline of Orange Street. He was a very good shortstop when he played baseball on the sandlot at North and Orange Streets, and he enjoyed swimming in the river with his friend David.

➤

SOUTHERN FRIED CHICKEN

2	cups flour
2	teaspoons salt
2	teaspoons pepper
2	teaspoons paprika
2	eggs
2	cups milk
2	cups shortening
3	tablespoons bacon drippings
2	chickens, cut up

Mix the flour, salt, pepper and paprika in a large plastic food storage bag. Beat the eggs and milk in a bowl. Melt the shortening and bacon drippings in a cast-iron skillet over medium heat. Heat until the mixture is sizzling. Dip each piece of chicken in the egg mixture. Place in the flour mixture and shake well. Remove the chicken to a rack and let stand for 5 minutes. Place the chicken in the hot shortening mixture; do not crowd the chicken pieces. Fry each piece on each side for 12 minutes or until golden brown. Yield: 8 servings.

Years later, when President Wilson died, it was his childhood friend, Edwin Anderson Alderman, who was chosen to give a memorial oration to both houses of Congress. Mr. Alderman, who served as president of the Universities of North Carolina and Virginia and of Tulane University, had studied catechism with "Tommy" while they were members of First Presbyterian Church.

CHICKEN PIE

1	(2- to 3-pound) chicken
6	tablespoons margarine
6	tablespoons flour
1	teaspoon salt
1/8	teaspoon pepper
1	cup evaporated milk
·	Biscuit Topping

Cook the chicken in water to cover in a large stockpot until tender. Remove the chicken to a plate to cool. Tear the chicken into bite-size pieces, discarding the skin and bones. Skim the top of the broth and discard. Reserve 3 cups of the broth. Melt the margarine in a saucepan. Stir in the flour, salt and pepper. Add the reserved broth, whisking constantly until smooth. Cook for 1 minute or until thickened, whisking constantly. Add the evaporated milk and chicken. Cook until heated through. Pour into a greased baking dish. Top with Biscuit Topping. Bake at 450 degrees for 10 minutes or until the top is golden brown. Yield: 6 to 8 servings.

Note: Prepare the chicken and store the bite-size chicken pieces covered with the broth in the refrigerator for 8 to 10 hours for moister chicken to use in the pie.

BISCUIT TOPPING

2	cups self-rising flour, sifted
1	teaspoon salt
1/3	cup shortening
2/3	cup milk or buttermilk

Mix the flour and salt in a bowl. Cut in the shortening with a fork until crumbly. Pour in the milk, stirring constantly just until mixed. The mixture will be moist; do not overwork the dough. Turn onto a lightly floured surface. Press the dough lightly with lightly floured hands. Roll into a circle 1/2 inch thick with a lightly floured rolling pin. Cut with a biscuit cutter.

Note: Omit the salt if using biscuits for something other than meat pies.

CHICKEN WITH SZECHUAN PEPPER SAUCE

1	(3½-pound) chicken
2	tablespoons crushed Szechuan peppercorns or Szechuan pepper blend
2	tablespoons kosher salt
1	cup chicken broth
1	tablespoon vegetable oil
¼	cup chopped green onions
1	tablespoon grated fresh gingerroot, or 1 teaspoon ground ginger
3	cloves of garlic, finely chopped
3	tablespoons vodka (optional)
2	tablespoons balsamic vinegar
1	tablespoon soy sauce

Remove the neck and giblets from the chicken. Rinse the chicken and pat dry with a paper towel. Rub the chicken with a mixture of the Szechuan peppercorns and salt. Place breast side up on a rack in a large roasting pan. Add ½ cup of the chicken broth to the pan. Bake at 375 degrees for 1 hour or until a meat thermometer inserted into the thigh without touching the bone registers 180 degrees, adding remaining chicken broth as needed. Remove the chicken to a serving platter, reserving the drippings. Let the chicken stand for 15 minutes. Skim the reserved pan drippings. Heat the vegetable oil in a small skillet. Add the green onions, ginger and garlic. Cook over medium heat for 2 minutes or until the green onions are softened. Stir in the vodka, balsamic vinegar, soy sauce and reserved pan drippings. Keep warm. Carve the chicken into serving pieces and serve with the sauce. Yield: 6 servings.

CHICKEN ALOUETTE

Such an impressive presentation—your guests will never know how easy it is to prepare this recipe.

1	(17-ounce) package frozen puff pastry, thawed
4	ounces garlic and spice Alouette cheese
6	boneless skinless chicken breasts
1/2	teaspoon salt
1/8	teaspoon pepper
1	egg, beaten
1	tablespoon water

Unfold the pastry sheets. Roll each sheet into a 12x14-inch rectangle on a lightly floured surface. Cut one of the pastry sheets into four 6x7-inch rectangles. Cut the remaining pastry sheet into two 6x7-inch rectangles and one 6x12-inch rectangle. Shape each 6x7-inch rectangle into an oval by trimming off the corners. Spread the pastry ovals evenly with the cheese. Sprinkle the chicken with salt and pepper. Place 1 chicken breast in the center of each pastry oval. Moisten the edges of the ovals with water. Fold the ends over the chicken; fold over the sides and press to seal. Place the chicken bundles seam side down on a lightly greased baking sheet. Cut the remaining large rectangle into 1/4x12-inch strips. Braid 2 of the strips together and place crosswise over the chicken bundles, trimming and reserving excess braid. Braid 2 of the strips and place lengthwise over the bundles, trimming and tucking the ends under. Repeat with the remaining strips and chicken bundles. Chill, covered, for up to 2 hours. Brush each pastry bundle with a mixture of the egg and water. Bake at 400 degrees on the lowest oven rack for 25 minutes or until golden brown. May substitute 1/2 cup chives-and-onion cream cheese for the Alouette cheese. Yield: 6 servings.

FETA CHICKEN

8	ounces rotini
4	chicken breasts, boned, cubed
2	teaspoons olive oil
2	medium onions, chopped
2	ribs celery, chopped
2	cloves of garlic, minced
1	(28-ounce) can peeled tomatoes
8	ounces feta cheese, cubed
·	Salt and pepper to taste
·	Chopped olives

Cook the pasta using the package directions; drain. Place the pasta in a large stockpot and cover with the lid. Sauté the chicken in the olive oil in a skillet until tender. Arrange the chicken over the pasta and cover. Add the onions, celery and garlic to the skillet. Sauté until the vegetables are soft. Add the undrained tomatoes. Cook until the liquid is reduced by half. Add to the stockpot. Stir in the feta cheese, salt and pepper. Cook over medium heat until heated through and a portion of the feta cheese is melted, stirring occasionally. Sprinkle with chopped olives.
Yield: 6 servings.

CHICKEN PESTO PIZZA

1/3	cup Pesto	1/2	cup coarsely chopped sun-
1	Homemade Pizza Crust		dried tomatoes
2	cups shredded Italian-blend	1/4	cup minced green onions
	cheese	·	Crushed red pepper flakes
2	blackened chicken breasts,		to taste
	cooked, chopped		

Spread the Pesto on the Homemade Pizza Crust. Sprinkle with 1/2 of the cheese. Add layers of the chicken, tomatoes and remaining cheese. Sprinkle with the green onions and red pepper flakes. Bake at 450 degrees for 10 minutes or until the cheese melts. Yield: 4 servings.

PESTO

2	cups firmly packed basil	2	tablespoons pine nuts,
	leaves		toasted
2	tablespoons each grated	3	cloves of garlic, minced
	Parmesan cheese and	1/2	to 1 cup olive oil
	Romano cheese	·	Salt and pepper to taste

Process the first 5 ingredients in a food processor until a paste forms. Add the olive oil gradually, processing at low speed until smooth. Stir in salt and pepper.

HOMEMADE PIZZA CRUST

1	envelope rapid-rise yeast	1	teaspoon salt
1/4	cup warm water	2	tablespoons olive oil
1	tablespoon honey	3	cups bread flour

Dissolve the yeast in 1/4 cup warm water. Mix the honey, salt and olive oil in a 1-cup glass measure. Add enough water to measure 1 cup. Place the bread flour in a food processor container. Add the yeast mixture and honey mixture in a fine stream, processing constantly until the mixture forms a ball. Place in a greased bowl, turning to coat the surface. Chill, covered, for 2 to 24 hours. Roll the dough into a circle on a lightly floured surface. Place in a pizza pan greased with olive oil. Bake at 400 degrees for 15 to 20 minutes or until the crust is golden brown.

CAROLINA TURKEY PIE

A blue-ribbon winner in the North Carolina Turkey Association bake-off, this is a great recipe to use for the leftover Thanksgiving turkey.

1	(10-ounce) can cream of celery soup
2	cups turkey broth
3/4	cup self-rising cornmeal
1	cup self-rising flour
1/2	teaspoon poultry seasoning
1/2	teaspoon pepper
1	teaspoon dried sage
2	tablespoons chopped onion
1 1/2	cups milk or buttermilk
1/2	cup melted margarine
4	cups chopped cooked turkey

Bring the celery soup and broth to a boil in a saucepan. Combine the cornmeal, self-rising flour, poultry seasoning, pepper and sage in a bowl and mix well. Stir in the onion. Add the buttermilk and margarine and mix well. Place the turkey in a greased 9x13-inch baking dish. Pour the broth mixture over the turkey. Spread the cornmeal mixture over the top. Bake at 425 degrees for 25 minutes or until brown. Yield: 8 servings.

Among Wilmington's more than
two hundred churches, St.
Mary Church is a fascinating
architectural creation built
entirely without nails, steel,
wood beams, or framing.
The Spanish Baroque cathedral
(1908–11) of brick and tile has
twin towers and a high dome
built over the design of a Greek
cross. The self-supporting dome,
built without scaffolding, is
an engineering masterpiece—
the workers stood on their
previous day's work.
Spanish architect Raphael
Gustavino, who worked on the
Vanderbilt House in Asheville,
North Carolina, died while
working on the church; his son
completed the commission.

►

STUFFED FLOUNDER

Serve with your favorite hollandaise sauce.

1	cup minced onions
1/2	cup minced green onions
1 1/2	cups minced celery
3	cloves of garlic, minced
1/5	bunch parsley, chopped
1	cup margarine
2	tablespoons flour
1	cup milk
1	cup dry white wine
1/2	cup chopped peeled boiled shrimp
1/2	cup crab meat
2 1/2	cups bread crumbs
·	Salt and pepper to taste
6	(1-pound) flounder, dressed

Sauté the onions, green onions, celery, garlic and parsley in the margarine in a skillet until the onions are transparent. Add the flour and blend well. Stir in the milk and wine gradually. Cook until thickened, stirring constantly. Stir in the shrimp and crab meat. Stir in the bread crumbs. Season with salt and pepper. Fill each flounder with the stuffing mixture. Arrange in a nonstick baking dish. Bake at 350 degrees for 20 minutes or until the fish is cooked through. Preheat the broiler. Broil for a few minutes or until the topping is brown. Yield: 6 servings.

BAKED SESAME MAHIMAHI

2	eggs
2	tablespoons milk
1	tablespoon lemon juice
1/2	teaspoon dry mustard
1/2	teaspoon salt
1/2	teaspoon pepper
1 1/2	pounds mahimahi fillets, skinned
1/2	cup flour
1	cup sesame seeds
6	tablespoons melted butter

Beat the eggs lightly in a bowl. Blend in the milk, lemon juice, dry mustard, salt and pepper. Dip the fish into the egg mixture; dredge in the flour. Dip into the egg mixture again. Place in a shallow layer of sesame seeds, turning and pressing until all sides of the fish are coated. Place the fish in 4 tablespoons of the melted butter in a baking dish. Pour the remaining 2 tablespoons butter over the top. Bake at 375 degrees for 15 minutes. Turn the fish over. Bake for 10 minutes longer or until the fish flakes easily. Yield: 4 servings.

On April 28, 1912, St. Mary Church was consecrated and dedicated by James Gibbons, Cardinal of the Roman Catholic Church. This visit to Wilmington was one of nostalgia for him; Gibbons had served as vicar apostolic of North Carolina at Wilmington's St. Thomas Church from 1868 to 1872.

BAKED RED SNAPPER

1/4	cup minced celery
2	tablespoons margarine
2	tablespoons chopped fresh tomato
2	tablespoons chopped fresh parsley
3	to 4 drops of Tabasco sauce
1/8	teaspoon thyme
·	Salt to taste
2	to 3 cups seasoned bread stuffing mix
1	(3- to 5-pound) red snapper, dressed
3	tablespoons margarine
·	Juice of 1 1/2 lemons
3	tablespoons Worcestershire sauce
3	to 5 dashes of Tabasco sauce
1 1/2	teaspoons salt
3/4	cup vegetable oil

Sauté the celery in 2 tablespoons margarine in a skillet until transparent. Add the tomato, parsley, Tabasco sauce, thyme and salt to taste and mix well. Stir in 2 cups of the stuffing mix. Stir in enough of the remaining stuffing mix to make the mixture of the desired consistency. Place the fish in a roasting pan. Fill the fish with the stuffing mixture.

Melt the margarine in a small saucepan. Stir in the lemon juice, Worcestershire sauce, Tabasco sauce and 1 1/2 teaspoons salt. Add the oil a small amount at a time, beating constantly. Pour over the stuffed fish. Bake at 350 degrees for 1 hour or until the fish flakes easily, basting frequently with the pan drippings. May use 3 to 5 pounds red snapper fillets, layering 1/2 of the fillets, stuffing mixture and remaining fillets in the baking dish and continuing as above. Yield: 6 to 8 servings.

SWORDFISH IN CREOLE MUSTARD SAUCE

2	cups fish stock or clam juice
1	cup whipping cream
2	tablespoons Creole mustard or coarsely ground French mustard
6	(8-ounce) swordfish steaks, 1 inch thick
½	cup olive oil
2	tablespoons minced fresh thyme
•	Minced fresh parsley to taste

Boil the stock in a heavy medium saucepan until reduced by half. Stir in the cream. Boil until the mixture is thick enough to coat the back of a spoon. Whisk in the mustard. Keep warm over low heat; do not boil. Brush the fish with the olive oil. Sprinkle with the thyme. Place on a grill rack. Grill for 9 minutes or until the fish flakes easily, turning once. Spoon the sauce onto each serving plate. Top with the fish. Sprinkle with parsley. Yield: 6 servings.

GRILLED FRESH TUNA WITH HERBS

⅓	cup olive oil
6	sprigs of fresh thyme
4	cloves of garlic, crushed
3	tablespoons fresh lemon juice
4	strips lemon peel
¼	teaspoon red pepper flakes
2	pounds fresh tuna
·	Freshly ground black pepper to taste
2	tablespoons butter
·	Lemon wedges
·	Parsley flakes
·	Parsley Butter

Combine the olive oil, thyme, garlic, lemon juice, lemon peel and red pepper flakes in a shallow dish. Sprinkle the tuna with black pepper on both sides. Place in the marinade. Marinate for 15 minutes. Drain the tuna, reserving the marinade. Place the tuna fatty side down on a grill rack. Grill for 5 to 6 minutes or until the tuna flakes easily, turning frequently. Bring the reserved marinade to a boil in a saucepan. Boil for 1 to 2 minutes. Stir in the butter until melted. Pour into a shallow dish. Add the grilled tuna, turning to coat both sides. Cut the tuna into thin slices. Garnish with lemon wedges and parsley flakes. Serve with a slice of Parsley Butter. Yield: 4 to 6 servings.

PARSLEY BUTTER

½	cup butter, softened
½	teaspoon salt
⅛	teaspoon pepper
2	tablespoons finely chopped fresh parsley
1	tablespoon fresh lemon juice

Beat the butter in a mixer bowl. Beat in the salt, pepper and parsley. Add the lemon juice 1 drop at a time, beating well after each addition. Shape the butter mixture into a cylinder 1 inch thick on a piece of waxed paper. Wrap in the waxed paper. Chill in the refrigerator. Yield: ½ cup.

CRAB MEAT AU GRATIN

1	tablespoon butter
1	tablespoon flour
1	cup half-and-half
·	Salt and pepper to taste
1	cup sherry, or to taste
1	pound white crab meat, drained, flaked
8	ounces New York sharp cheese, sliced

Melt the butter over hot water in a double boiler. Add the flour and stir until smooth. Add the half-and-half. Cook until thickened and smooth, stirring constantly. Season with salt and pepper. Stir in the sherry. Stir in the crab meat gently. Cook until the crab meat is heated through. Spoon into a baking dish or individual ramekins. Cover with the cheese slices. Bake at 325 degrees until heated through. Broil until the cheese melts and is light brown. Serve immediately. Yield: 4 to 6 servings.

In the early 1900s, Mr. Pembroke Jones of Wrightsville Sound was known for his extravagant parties. His guest list included members of the social register: the Astors, the Vanderbilts, the Whitneys, and the Belmonts. But on one particular occasion, it wasn't his lavish Italian Villa in Pembroke Park or his country estate in Airlie Gardens where he chose to entertain. Mr. W. C. Taylor, his park superintendent, recalled the time he used the massive limbs of an old live oak to support a platform for a dining table, complete with white linens and silver. Guests reached the dinner party by climbing a winding railed staircase that encircled the trunk of the lovely old tree.

BAKED CRAB MEAT CASSEROLE

1	cup Pepperidge Farm dried stuffing
·	Milk
4	hard-cooked eggs, chopped
1	cup mayonnaise
1	teaspoon Worcestershire sauce
1	teaspoon lemon juice
1/2	teaspoon cayenne
1	pound crab meat, drained, flaked
·	Bread crumbs
·	Pats of butter

Place the stuffing in a glass measure. Add enough milk to measure 1 cup. Mix with the chopped eggs, mayonnaise, Worcestershire sauce, lemon juice and cayenne in a large bowl. Stir in the crab meat gently. Spoon into a buttered baking dish. Sprinkle generously with bread crumbs and dot with butter. Bake at 350 degrees for 20 to 30 minutes or until heated through. Yield: 8 servings.

CAPE FEAR CRAB CAKES WITH LEMON DILL SAUCE

1	pound fresh lump crab meat
1	tablespoon butter
1	clove of garlic, minced
1	scallion, finely chopped
2	tablespoons finely chopped red bell pepper
3	tablespoons whipping cream
1	tablespoon Dijon mustard
·	Cayenne to taste
1	egg, beaten
1	teaspoon each minced fresh basil and parsley
1	cup fine dry bread crumbs
1/4	cup grated Parmesan cheese
2	tablespoons each butter and vegetable oil
·	Lemon Dill Sauce

Flake the crab meat and remove bits of shell and cartilage. Melt 1 tablespoon butter in a large skillet. Add the garlic, scallion and red pepper. Sauté for 2 minutes or until tender. Stir in the whipping cream, mustard and cayenne. Remove from the heat. Let stand until slightly cool. Add the egg, basil, parsley, 1/2 cup of the bread crumbs and the crab meat and mix lightly. Shape into 16 patties 2 inches in diameter. Mix the remaining 1/2 cup bread crumbs and Parmesan cheese in a shallow dish. Dredge the patties in the crumb mixture until coated. Place on a platter. Chill, covered, for 1 hour or longer. Melt 2 tablespoons butter and oil in a large skillet over medium heat. Add the patties. Fry for 3 minutes on each side. Drain on paper towels. Serve with Lemon Dill Sauce. Yield: 16 servings.

LEMON DILL SAUCE

3/4	cup mayonnaise
1/2	cup buttermilk
1	clove of garlic, minced
2	tablespoons chopped fresh dillweed
1	tablespoon chopped fresh parsley
1	tablespoon grated lemon peel
2	teaspoons fresh lemon juice

Blend the mayonnaise and buttermilk in a bowl until smooth. Add the garlic, dillweed, parsley, lemon peel and lemon juice and mix well. Chill, covered, in the refrigerator until the mixture thickens.

Of the millions of people who visit the Lincoln Memorial in Washington, D.C., few know that the monument's foundation is designed after The Rocks in Wilmington. Architect Henry Bacon, who won the design competition for the Memorial in 1912, spent his youth in Wilmington while his father, an engineer, supervised construction of The Rocks, a barrier closing off New Inlet from the sea. In Wilmington, in 1901, Bacon designed the exceptional brick and shingle Donald MacRae house on South Third Street, now owned by St. James Church.

►

MOULES MARINIÈRES

6	pints fresh mussels, scrubbed
4	small onions, chopped
2	tablespoons butter
4	sprigs of parsley
¼	teaspoon thyme
1	bay leaf
1	cup dry white wine
·	Chopped fresh parsley to taste
·	Freshly ground pepper

Discard any mussels that are not tightly closed. Sauté the onions in melted butter in a large saucepan until soft. Add the sprigs of parsley, thyme, bay leaf, wine and mussels. Cook, covered, for 3 minutes. Shake the saucepan. Cook for 3 minutes longer. Remove the mussels to a serving dish using a slotted spoon and cover to keep warm. Cook the sauce until reduced to the desired consistency, stirring occasionally. Remove the sprigs of parsley and bay leaf. Pour the sauce over the mussels. Sprinkle with chopped parsley and pepper. Yield: 6 to 8 servings.

SCALLOP KABOBS

6	limes, sliced
3	pounds scallops
8	ounces Canadian bacon, sliced
1/2	cup butter, melted
6	tablespoons grated Parmesan cheese

Reserve several of the lime slices and set aside. Alternate the scallops, remaining lime slices and Canadian bacon slices on skewers. Squeeze the juice from the reserved lime slices over the scallops. Coat the scallops generously with 1/2 of the melted butter. Sprinkle with 1/2 of the Parmesan cheese. Place the skewers on a hot grill rack 4 inches from the heat source. Grill for 6 to 7 minutes. Turn the skewers and brush with the remaining melted butter and sprinkle with the remaining Parmesan cheese. Grill for 6 to 7 minutes longer. Yield: 6 servings.

In 1915 Bacon also designed Live Oaks, the Walter Parsley residence on Masonboro Sound. The white octagonal house, surrounded by spacious green lawns and live oak trees, is a unique portrait of coastal living. Henry Bacon is buried in Wilmington's Oakdale Cemetery.

SHRIMP-STUFFED ARTICHOKE BOATS

4¹/₂	quarts water
2	tablespoons olive oil
2	cloves of garlic, thinly sliced
1	teaspoon salt
1	teaspoon sugar
6	medium artichokes
2	tablespoons olive oil
¹/₂	teaspoon minced garlic
1	pound medium shrimp, peeled, deveined, chopped
¹/₄	cup chopped green onions
¹/₂	teaspoon salt
¹/₂	teaspoon pepper
1	cup fresh bread crumbs
¹/₄	cup chopped fresh parsley
2	teaspoons fresh lemon juice

Bring the water, 2 tablespoons olive oil, sliced garlic, 1 teaspoon salt and sugar to a boil in a Dutch oven. Cut the tops and stems off the artichokes. Snip off the tips of the leaves with scissors. Add the artichokes to the boiling water mixture. Return to a boil and reduce the heat. Simmer, covered, for 25 minutes or until a leaf near the center of the artichokes pulls out easily. Drain and let stand until cool. Remove the center leaves of the artichokes. Scrape out the fuzzy centers and discard. Heat 2 tablespoons olive oil in a skillet. Add the minced garlic. Cook for 1 minute. Add the shrimp, green onions, ¹/₂ teaspoon salt and pepper. Cook for 3 to 4 minutes or until the shrimp turns pink, stirring constantly. Remove from the heat. Stir in the bread crumbs, parsley and lemon juice. Spoon about ¹/₃ cup shrimp stuffing into each artichoke. Arrange in a greased 9x13-inch glass baking dish. Bake, covered with foil, at 325 degrees for 20 minutes. Yield: 6 servings.

SHRIMP CREOLE

½	cup chopped celery
½	cup chopped onion
⅔	cup chopped green bell pepper
¼	cup butter
2	tablespoons minced fresh parsley
3	tablespoons flour
3	(14-ounce) cans crushed tomatoes
1	teaspoon salt
¼	teaspoon pepper
3	tablespoons Worcestershire sauce
1	clove of garlic, crushed
⅓	teaspoon paprika
1	tablespoon lemon juice
1	teaspoon celery seeds
2	bay leaves
·	Tabasco sauce to taste
1	pound shrimp, peeled, deveined
1½	cups rice, cooked

Sauté the celery, onion and green pepper in the butter in a skillet until golden brown. Add the parsley and flour and mix well. Add the tomatoes, salt, pepper, Worcestershire sauce, garlic, paprika, lemon juice, celery seeds, bay leaves and Tabasco sauce and mix well. Stir in the shrimp. Cook over low heat for 10 minutes. Remove the bay leaves. Spoon over the hot cooked rice. Yield: 6 servings.

From 1905 to the 1930s, thousands of people rode the trolley to Wrightsville Beach to dance at Lumina Pavilion. Called the "Beautiful Palace of Light" and "Pleasure Palace of the South," this massive three-story wooden structure boasted a six-thousand-square-foot ballroom with an acoustically perfect orchestra shell. The best bands played as patrons danced on the gleaming wooden dance floor or observed the dancers from the promenade. One visitor recalled the romance of watching silent movies from the third floor deck outside over the waves, while sailors remember Lumina's glowing silhouette as a welcome beacon.

SHRIMP AND GRITS

2	large white onions, chopped
1	large green bell pepper, chopped
6	tablespoons bacon drippings
2	pounds medium shrimp, boiled, peeled, deveined
1	cup (about) water
1/4	cup flour
1/4	cup water
1	tablespoon Worcestershire sauce
1/4	cup tomato chili sauce
1	teaspoon salt
·	Pepper to taste
·	Hot cooked grits

Sauté the onions and green pepper in the bacon drippings in a large skillet until the onions are golden brown. Stir in the shrimp. Add just enough of the 1 cup water to make a sauce; do not cover the shrimp. Simmer for 3 minutes. Stir in a mixture of the flour and 1/4 cup water. Cook until thickened, stirring constantly. Add the Worcestershire sauce, chili sauce, salt and pepper and mix well. Cook until of the desired consistency, stirring frequently. Spoon over the hot grits.
Yield: 4 servings.

GRILLED SHRIMP WITH SWEET-AND-SOUR DIPPING SAUCE

2	pounds large or jumbo shrimp
1	cup vegetable oil
1	cup lemon juice
2	teaspoons Italian salad dressing mix
2	teaspoons seasoned salt
1	teaspoon freshly ground pepper
1	teaspoon Worcestershire sauce
1/4	cup packed brown sugar
2	tablespoons soy sauce
1/2	cup chopped green onions

Rinse the shrimp well. Peel and devein the shrimp. Drain on paper towels. Mix the vegetable oil, lemon juice, salad dressing mix, seasoned salt, pepper and Worcestershire sauce in a bowl. Place the shrimp in a large bowl. Add the marinade. Marinate, covered, in the refrigerator for 2 to 4 hours, stirring occasionally. Drain the shrimp, reserving the marinade. Bring the reserved marinade to a boil in a saucepan. Boil for 1 to 2 minutes. Thread the shrimp onto skewers and place on a hot grill rack. Grill for 7 to 10 minutes, turning once and brushing with some of the heated marinade. Add the brown sugar, soy sauce and green onions to the remaining marinade. Bring to a boil. Boil for 1 to 2 minutes, stirring frequently. Serve with the shrimp for dipping. Yield: 8 servings.

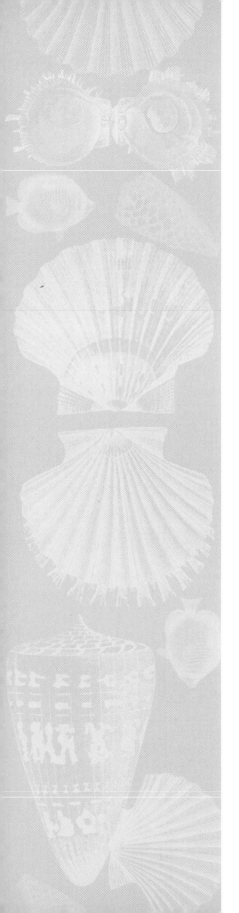

A Memory

Robert Ruark (1915–1965), author from the Lower Cape Fear, commanded international attention and was compared to Ernest Hemingway. His autobiographical novel *The Old Man and the Boy* described his memories.

We were living at a place called Wrightsville Sound that spring, a most

fascinating spot to be young in . . . The Sound itself led to two inlets on

a beach two miles away . . . There's something about a boat that is

powerful soothing to springtime hysterics . . . Ain't nothing like a boat

to teach a man the worth of quiet contemplation . . . I think I must

have known every inch of that Sound, every fish hole, every sandbar,

every creek and cove. I knew the tricks of the tides around the inlets and

the rate the water would drop, according to how the wind was blowing.

It was all trial and error, cut feet, bruised fingers, mosquitoes and

sandflies and sunburn . . . By the end of the summer I was considerably

calmed down . . . there is nothing like being alone on the water in a boat

of your own to learn the value of peace, quiet, and responsibility.

—Robert Chester Ruark, 1957

Excerpted from *Carolina Yacht Club Chronicles*, by Anne Russell.

BARBECUED DOVE BREAST

  24   to 240 dove breasts
-     Vinegar
  1   to 6 bottles honey
-     Carolina Treet or other cooking sauce

Place the doves in water to cover in a large pan. Add 1 cup vinegar to every gallon of water used. Soak in the refrigerator for 1 hour to overnight. Coat each dove with honey. Preheat one side of a two-burner grill to high and the other side to medium. Place the coated doves breast side up on the rack over the high heat. Cook until the breast bones are charred. Dip in Carolina Treet. Place on the rack over the medium heat. Grill until the doves are cooked through. Yield: Variable.

Greenfield Park was first known in the late 1700s as Greenfield Plantation. Later called McIlhenney's Mill Pond, the lake became a favorite swimming hole for Wilmington youth at the turn of the century. The one-hundred-thirty-acre cypress lake and surrounding twenty acres of camellias, dogwoods, azaleas, and crape myrtles was purchased by the city in 1925. When the Depression set in, the people of Wilmington banded together and privately financed the building of the five-mile community drive around the park. The citizens raised $110,000 and put more than fifteen hundred people to work. Both rich and poor were crucial to the successful campaign.

When Hurricane Hazel hit the Cape Fear Coast, it caught a young honeymoon couple off guard. They awoke on October 15, 1954, to one-hundred-fifty-mile-per-hour winds and water lapping at their first floor. Breaking into a sturdier cottage, they stayed until the water rose to the second floor. Realizing the building would soon collapse, they floated a mattress out the window with the bride tied on, because she couldn't swim.

➤

DUCK KIEV

4	whole duck breasts
2	tablespoons chopped chives
2	tablespoons chopped parsley
1	tablespoon minced garlic
1/2	teaspoon salt
1/4	teaspoon white pepper
8	tablespoons butter
3	eggs, beaten
·	Flour
·	Cracker crumbs
·	Vegetable oil for deep-frying

Debone the duck breasts and remove the skin. Cut the duck breasts into halves. Pound 1/4 inch thick. Mix the chives, parsley, garlic, salt and white pepper in a bowl. Roll each tablespoon of butter in the seasoning mixture. Place 1 coated butter slice in the center of 1 duck breast. Wrap around the butter and secure with a wooden pick. Dip in the beaten egg and roll in the flour. Dip in the beaten eggs again and roll in the cracker crumbs. Repeat with the remaining butter and duck breasts. Deep-fry in hot vegetable oil in a deep fryer for 5 to 10 minutes or until golden brown and cooked through. Yield: 4 (2-piece) servings.

QUAIL WITH WINE SAUCE

Serve the extra sauce from this simple and elegant recipe over wild rice.

2	small onions, chopped
2	whole cloves
1	teaspoon peppercorns
2	cloves of garlic, chopped
½	bay leaf
½	cup butter
6	quail
2	cups white wine
½	teaspoon salt
¼	teaspoon black pepper
·	Cayenne to taste
1	teaspoon chives
2	cups evaporated milk

Sauté the onions, cloves, peppercorns, garlic and bay leaf in the butter in a skillet until the onions are transparent. Add the quail. Cook until the quail are brown. Add the wine, salt, black pepper, cayenne and chives. Simmer for 30 minutes. Remove the quail to a serving dish. Strain the pan drippings and return to the skillet. Stir in the evaporated milk. Bring to a boil, stirring constantly. Pour over the quail. Yield: 6 servings.

Their makeshift boat became wedged in the top of an oak tree across the sound, where they rode out the storm. The next day the couple returned to Long Beach; of three hundred fifty-seven buildings, all but five were destroyed. Their cottage was gone but they found their refrigerator with wedding cake and Champagne intact. There the newlyweds celebrated.

BLACKENED VENISON TENDERLOIN

·	Wild Game Marinade (page 137)
·	Meat tenderizer to taste
1	clove of garlic, chopped
1	venison tenderloin
1	teaspoon chili powder
1/4	teaspoon cayenne
1/2	teaspoon tarragon
1	teaspoon paprika
1/2	teaspoon rosemary
2	tablespoons lemon juice
1	tablespoon olive oil
1	clove of garlic, chopped

Combine the Wild Game Marinade, meat tenderizer and 1 clove of garlic in a shallow glass dish. Add the venison. Marinate, covered, in the refrigerator for 8 to 10 hours; drain. Coat the venison with a mixture of the chili powder, cayenne, tarragon, paprika and rosemary. Heat the lemon juice, olive oil and 1 clove of garlic in a 9-inch cast-iron skillet over medium-high heat. Add the venison. Cook until blackened on all sides. Reduce the heat to low. Cook for 30 minutes or until of the desired degree of doneness, covering for 30 seconds at a time. Cut into thin slices. Serve with horseradish sauce. Yield: 2 servings.

WILD GAME MARINADE

2   cups cider vinegar

·   Juice of 3 lemons

1   (10-ounce) bottle Worcestershire sauce

1   (5-ounce) bottle Tabasco sauce

1/4   cup soy sauce

1/2   cup red wine

2   tablespoons brown sugar

2   tablespoons salt

2   tablespoons pepper

Combine the vinegar, lemon juice, Worcestershire sauce, Tabasco sauce, soy sauce, red wine, brown sugar, salt and pepper in a container with a tightfitting lid and mix well. Store, tightly covered, in the refrigerator. May use the green Tabasco sauce when using as a marinade for mild-flavored game. Yield: 4½ to 5 cups.

Concerts, garden parties, historic-mansion tours, and garden tours have been a tradition since the festival began in 1948. Many celebrities have been associated with the festival, among them President Ronald Reagan, who served as emcee in 1959.

Desserts

A flower-filled garden in Wilmington provides a lush backdrop for outdoor entertaining. Desserts are a favorite for every occasion. Often, the most simple recipe can be the most luscious and elegant—as the Summer Jewel recipe. When fresh strawberries are "in," people all over the South feel inspired to have a party. Whether you serve Strawberries Sabayon, or just simple unadorned juicy berries, sampling the fresh fruits of each season allows dieters and indulgers alike to enjoy dessert.

CHAMPION APPLE COBBLER

½	cup butter or margarine
2	cups sugar
2	cups water
½	cup shortening
1½	cups sifted self-rising flour
⅓	cup milk
3	cups finely chopped tart apples (4 apples)
1	teaspoon cinnamon

Melt the butter in a 9x13-inch baking pan in a 350-degree oven. Heat the sugar and water in a saucepan until the sugar is dissolved, stirring frequently. Cut the shortening into the flour in a bowl until crumbly. Add the milk and stir until the dough leaves the side of the bowl. Knead on a floured surface until smooth. Roll the dough into a large rectangle ¼ inch thick. Layer the apples evenly over the dough. Sprinkle with the cinnamon. Roll up as for a jelly roll. Cut into 16 slices ½ inch thick. Arrange in the prepared pan. Pour the sugar syrup around the rolls. Bake for 55 to 60 minutes. May decrease the amount of sugar in the sugar syrup, but always use 2 cups of liquid. May substitute other fruit for the apples. Yield: 16 servings.

Note: Substitute ½ cup fresh orange juice for ½ cup of the water and add 3 tablespoons fresh lemon juice if the apples are fairly sweet.

On "Black Thursday" in 1955, the Atlantic Coast Line Railroad announced its closing. By 1960 the Railroad relocated four thousand Wilmington families to Jacksonville, Florida. Vacant downtown mansions and buildings stood in disrepair. In 1960, Wilmingtonians made another start. The city has one of the earliest nominated historic districts in the state. By 1974 Wilmington became the state's largest urban historic district listed in the National Register of Historic Places.

GLAZED STRAWBERRY CREAM CHEESECAKE

3/4	cup (3 ounces) coarsely ground walnuts
3/4	cup finely ground graham crackers
3	tablespoons melted unsalted butter
2	cups sour cream
1/4	cup sugar
1	teaspoon vanilla extract
32	ounces cream cheese, softened
4	eggs
1 1/4	cups sugar
1	tablespoon lemon juice
2	teaspoons vanilla extract
1	quart strawberries, rinsed
·	Glaze

Combine the walnuts, graham crackers and butter in a bowl and mix well. Press into a lightly greased 9-inch springform pan. Blend the sour cream, 1/4 cup sugar and 1 teaspoon vanilla in a bowl. Chill, covered, in the refrigerator. Beat the cream cheese in a mixer bowl until smooth. Beat in the eggs, 1 1/4 cups sugar, lemon juice and 2 teaspoons vanilla. Spoon into the prepared springform pan. Place the springform pan on a baking sheet. Place on the center oven rack. Bake at 350 degrees for 50 to 55 minutes or until set. Let stand at room temperature for 15 minutes. Spoon the sour cream topping over the cheesecake. Bake for 5 minutes. Let stand until cool. Chill for 24 hours or preferably for 2 to 3 days. Loosen the cheesecake from the side of the pan and remove the side. Arrange the strawberries pointed end up on the top. Spoon the Glaze over the strawberries. Chill in the refrigerator until the Glaze is set. May bake in a 10-inch springform pan for 40 to 45 minutes or until set. Yield: 10 to 12 servings.

GLAZE

1	(12-ounce) jar raspberry jelly
1	tablespoon cornstarch
1/4	cup orange liqueur
1/4	cup water

Combine a small amount of the jelly with cornstarch in a saucepan and mix well. Add the remaining jelly, orange liqueur and water. Cook over medium heat for 5 minutes or until thickened and clear, stirring constantly. Cool to lukewarm.

Native Wilmingtonian and national journalist David Brinkley, addressing the Historic Wilmington Foundation in 1975, said: "We slept through the uglification of America and did not suffer the mutilation that has occurred in so many other cities. Its setting on the river, the ocean and the bays and sounds is exceptional." The collective vision of thousands of people restored a national treasure, making historic Wilmington a vibrant place in the twentieth century.

STRAWBERRY CREAM CREPES

1/4	cup sugar
2	pints strawberries, sliced
3	ounces cream cheese, softened
1	cup whipping cream
•	Sugar to taste
10	Crepes
1/3	cup brandy or kirsch

Sprinkle 1/4 cup sugar over the strawberries in a bowl and toss to coat well. Beat the cream cheese in a mixer bowl until smooth. Add the whipping cream gradually, beating until thick and smooth. Sweeten with sugar to taste. Place a dollop of the whipped cream mixture on each Crepe and roll up. Chill in the refrigerator. Place the strawberries in a chafing dish. Add the brandy and ignite. Arrange the crepes on serving plates. Spoon the sauce over the crepes. May omit the liquor and serve the strawberries over the cold crepes. Yield: 10 servings.

CREPES

1 1/2	cups sifted flour
1/3	cup sugar
1/8	teaspoon salt
5	eggs
2	cups milk
1/2	teaspoon vanilla extract
1/2	teaspoon orange zest
1/4	teaspoon lemon zest
2	tablespoons Cointreau
2	teaspoons clarified butter

Mix the flour, sugar and salt in a large bowl. Beat the eggs and milk in a bowl. Add to the flour mixture gradually, stirring until smooth. Add the vanilla, orange zest, lemon zest and Cointreau and mix well. Chill, covered, for 30 minutes. Coat a nonstick crepe pan with some of the clarified butter. Heat over medium heat until hot. Add 3 tablespoons of the batter, tilting the pan so the batter covers the bottom. Cook for 40 seconds or until light brown, turning once. Remove to a wire rack to cool. Repeat with the remaining batter and clarified butter. Stack the cooled crepes with waxed paper between each layer. Yield: 10 crepes.

CHARLOTTE AU CHOCOLATE

2   cups semisweet chocolate chips
6   egg whites
2   tablespoons sugar
6   egg yolks
2   cups whipping cream, whipped
4   dozen ladyfingers

Melt the chocolate chips in a double boiler over hot water. Let stand until cool. Beat the egg whites in a mixer bowl until soft peaks form. Add the sugar gradually, beating until stiff peaks form. Beat the egg yolks 1 at a time into the cooled chocolate. Beat in 1/4 of the stiffly beaten egg whites. Fold in the remaining stiffly beatened egg whites. Fold in the whipped cream. Line the bottom and side of a 9-inch springform pan with ladyfingers. Spoon 1/3 of the chocolate mixture into the prepared pan. Layer the remaining ladyfingers and remaining chocolate mixture 1/2 at a time over the chocolate mixture. Chill in the refrigerator for 4 hours or until firm. Remove the side of the springform pan and serve immediately.
Yield: 16 servings.

CLASSIC BANANA PUDDING

1   cup sugar
3   tablespoons flour
3   egg yolks
1/8   teaspoon vanilla extract
1   cup milk
4   bananas, sliced
40   vanilla wafers
3   egg whites
3   tablespoons sugar

Mix 1 cup sugar and flour in a bowl. Beat the egg yolks in a mixer bowl until thick and pale yellow. Add the sugar mixture gradually, beating constantly. Stir in the vanilla. Scald the milk in a skillet over medium heat. Stir in the egg yolk mixture. Cook until thickened, stirring constantly. Remove from the heat. Let stand until cool. Alternate layers of the pudding, bananas and vanilla wafers in a 1 1/2-quart baking dish until all of the ingredients are used. Beat the egg whites in a mixer bowl until soft peaks form. Add 3 tablespoons sugar gradually, beating constantly until stiff peaks form. Spread the meringue over the pudding, sealing to the edge. Bake at 450 degrees until the meringue is golden brown. Yield: 6 servings.

BREAD PUDDING WITH GRAND MARNIER SAUCE

This recipe takes a little extra time to prepare, but every bite is worth it.

1/2	cup unsalted butter, softened
1	cup sugar
5	eggs, beaten
1	pint whipping cream
1	tablespoon vanilla extract
1/8	teaspoon cinnamon
1/4	cup raisins
12	(1-inch-thick) slices fresh or dried French bread
·	Grand Marnier Sauce

Beat the butter and sugar in a mixer bowl until creamy. Add the eggs, whipping cream, vanilla and cinnamon and beat well. Stir in the raisins. Pour into a 9x9-inch baking pan. Arrange the bread slices over the top of the whipping cream mixture. Let stand for 5 minutes or until the bread has soaked up some of the mixture. Turn the bread over. Let stand for 10 minutes longer. Push the bread into the mixture so that most of the bread is submerged. Do not break up the slices. Set the pan in a larger pan. Pour enough water into the larger pan to reach 1/2 inch up the side of the inner pan. Bake, covered with foil, at 350 degrees for 35 minutes. Bake, uncovered, for 10 minutes longer or until the top is brown and the pudding is still soft. Spoon onto serving plates. Serve with Grand Marnier Sauce.
Yield: 9 servings.

GRAND MARNIER SAUCE

1/2	teaspoon cornstarch
1/4	cup water
1	cup whipping cream
1	cup sugar
1	tablespoon unsalted butter
1/8	teaspoon cinnamon
1	tablespoon Grand Marnier

Dissolve the cornstarch in the water in a bowl. Combine the whipping cream, sugar, butter and cinnamon in a medium saucepan. Bring to a boil over high heat. Cook for 3 minutes or until the sugar dissolves, stirring frequently. Stir in the cornstarch mixture. Cook for 3 minutes or until slightly thickened, stirring constantly. Remove from the heat. Stir in the Grand Marnier.

DEEP DARK SECRET

Generations ago this dessert was called Date Pudding and was steamed in a pudding mold. Dates and fresh fruits were not commonly available then, which made this an exotic treat. Serve this recipe during the holidays for a nice change from traditional fruitcake.

½	cup flour
1	teaspoon baking powder
¼	teaspoon salt
1	pound dates, chopped
4	egg yolks
1	cup sugar
1	cup chopped nuts
2	teaspoons vanilla extract
4	egg whites, stiffly beaten
1	pint whipping cream
·	Sugar to taste
4	bananas, sliced
1	(11-ounce) can mandarin oranges, drained
1	(20-ounce) can crushed pineapple
1	(4-ounce) bottle maraschino cherries, drained

Sift the flour, baking powder and salt together. Sprinkle the dates with a small amount of additional flour in a bowl and toss to coat. Beat the egg yolks in a mixer bowl. Add 1 cup sugar gradually, beating constantly after each addition. Blend in the sifted flour mixture. Fold in the dates, nuts and vanilla. Fold in the stiffly beaten egg whites. Spread in a greased 9x13-inch baking pan. Bake at 350 degrees for 30 minutes. Let stand until cool. Beat the whipping cream in a mixer bowl. Add sugar to taste, beating until soft peaks form. Break the cake into pieces. Arrange several cake pieces on individual dessert plates. Cover with sliced bananas and mandarin oranges. Add more cake pieces. Spoon undrained pineapple over the layers. Top with maraschino cherries. Frost with the sweetened whipped cream. Garnish with additional chopped cherries and chopped nuts. May assemble the dessert on a large dessert plate. Yield: 12 servings.

BAKED EGG CUSTARD

2	eggs
1/2	cup sugar
1/2	teaspoon salt
2	cups scalded milk
1/2	teaspoon vanilla extract
·	Nutmeg to taste

Beat the eggs, sugar and salt in a mixer bowl. Stir in the scalded milk and vanilla. Pour into custard cups. Place the cups in a baking pan containing 1 inch water. Bake at 325 degrees for 45 minutes or until set. Sprinkle with nutmeg. Yield: 6 servings.

CHAMPAGNE PEACH CUP

A divine light dessert to serve for a luncheon or a summer supper.

3	cups sliced fresh peaches
·	Sugar to taste
·	Juice of 1/2 lemon
6	tablespoons corn syrup
2	cups crushed ice
2	cups Champagne
·	Fresh peach slices

Process 3 cups peaches, sugar, lemon juice, corn syrup, ice and Champagne 1/2 at a time in a blender container. Pour into individual sherbet dishes. Garnish with fresh peach slices. May store in the freezer until serving time and process in the blender just before serving. May use two 10-ounce packages frozen peaches. May use simple syrup instead of corn syrup. Yield: 6 to 8 servings.

STRAWBERRIES SABAYON

30	to 36 fresh large strawberries
2	egg yolks
2	tablespoons sugar
2	tablespoons sherry, marsala or orange liqueur
1/4	cup confectioners' sugar
1	cup whipping cream

Rinse the strawberries in cold water and pat dry. Remove the stems from the strawberries. Cut each strawberry into quarters from the pointed end, cutting to but not through the strawberry. Chill in the refrigerator. Beat the egg yolks in the top of a double boiler. Add the sugar and sherry. Place over simmering water. Beat for 5 minutes or until thick and soft peaks form. Remove the top of the double boiler from the heat and place immediately into a bowl of ice. Continue beating for 2 minutes. Place the entire stack in the refrigerator. Chill for 30 minutes. Combine the confectioners' sugar and whipping cream in a bowl. Chill for 30 minutes. Add the chilled sabayon to the cream mixture and beat until the mixture is stiff. Place in a pastry bag fitted with a 1/2-inch star tip. Pipe into each strawberry. Chill in the refrigerator for up to 8 hours. May fill a sealable plastic food storage bag with the sabayon, cut off the tip of 1 corner and pipe into the strawberries. May prepare the sabayon cream 1 day in advance. Yield: 30 to 36 servings.

Note: Sabayon may be spooned into individual sherbet dishes and layered with sliced strawberries or other fresh fruit.

SUMMER JEWEL

An excellent party choice, this jewel-bright, luscious dessert is always a part of the dinner conversation.

1   cup bite-size pieces Fuji or Golden Delicious apple
1   cup melon balls
1   cup seedless grapes
1   cup chopped fresh peaches or plums
1   cup chopped fresh pears
1   cup pitted fresh Bing cherries
1½   cups sugar
1½   cups Cointreau, curaçao, Grand Marnier, amaretto, creme de menthe,
       cherry brandy or any favorite liqueur
1   whole cantaloupe or honeydew melon
·   Sprigs of fresh mint

Combine the apple, melon balls, grapes, peaches, pears and cherries in a large bowl and mix gently. Sprinkle with 1 cup of the sugar. Pour in 1 cup of the liqueur and mix lightly. Chill, covered, for 2 hours or longer. Peel the whole melon. Cut across the center into 8 rings and remove the seeds from each center. Place the melon rings in a 9x13-inch glass dish. Sprinkle with the remaining ½ cup sugar and ½ cup liqueur. Chill, covered, in the refrigerator. To serve, place a melon ring on each dessert plate. Spoon the mixed fruit into the center. Garnish with fresh mint. Yield: 8 servings.

Note: Serve the mixed fruit in a footed compote or individual stemmed sherbet dishes. Use any combination of fresh fruits in season. Allow ¾ cup fruit and 2 tablespoons each of sugar and liqueur for each serving.

MINT SHERBET

- 6 tablespoons chopped fresh mint leaves
- · Juice of 6 oranges
- · Juice of 2 lemons
- · Grated peel of 1 lemon
- 2 cups sugar
- 2 cups water
- · Few drops of green food coloring (optional)
- 1 egg white, stiffly beaten
- 1 cup whipping cream
- · Fresh sprigs of mint

Soak the chopped mint leaves in a mixture of the orange juice, lemon juice and lemon peel in a large bowl for 30 minutes. Bring the sugar and water to a boil in a saucepan. Boil for 5 minutes; do not stir. Add to the fruit juice mixture. Let stand until cool. Strain the mixture into a bowl. Tint with food coloring. Fold in the stiffly beaten egg white and whipping cream. Pour into an ice cream freezer container. Freeze using the manufacturer's instructions. Spoon into individual dessert dishes. Garnish with fresh mint sprigs. Yield: 6 to 8 servings.

When Wilmington was founded in the 1730s, a number of large creeks traversed the town, emptying into the Cape Fear River. The city had arches built over these waterways so as not to impede their flow, and as the town grew, the arches were covered with dirt and the city grew on top of them. These tunnels have been the object of many legends. Most famous of these, Jacob's Run is large enough to stand up in. Pirates, smugglers, and escaping slaves are said to have used it. In 1978 Cooperative Savings & Loan had to fill in a portion of this tunnel, which ran under the place where the new vault would be constructed.

APPLE CAKE WITH CARAMEL GLAZE

3	large eggs
2	cups sugar
1½	cups vegetable oil
3	cups flour
1	teaspoon baking soda
1	teaspoon salt
2	teaspoons vanilla extract
3	cups coarsely grated tart apples
1	cup chopped walnuts or pecans
·	Caramel Glaze

Combine the eggs, sugar and vegetable oil in a mixer bowl and beat well. Beat in the flour, baking soda, salt and vanilla. Fold in the apples and walnuts. Pour the batter into a greased 10-inch tube pan or 9x13-inch cake pan. Bake at 325 degrees for 1½ hours. Drizzle the Caramel Glaze over the warm cake. Let stand until cool. Remove to a cake plate. Yield: 15 to 16 servings.

CARAMEL GLAZE

½	cup butter or margarine
1	cup light brown sugar
¼	cup evaporated milk

Melt the butter in a saucepan. Stir in the brown sugar and evaporated milk. Bring to a boil. Boil for 2½ minutes.

BROWN MOUNTAIN CAKE

1	cup butter, softened
2	cups sugar
3	eggs
1	teaspoon vanilla extract
3	cups flour, sifted
1	cup buttermilk
3	tablespoons baking cocoa
1	teaspoon baking soda
1/2	cup warm water
•	Boiled Icing

Cream the butter and sugar in a mixer bowl until light and fluffy. Add the eggs 1 at a time, beating well after each addition. Beat in the vanilla. Add the sifted flour and buttermilk alternately, beating well after each addition. Dissolve the baking cocoa and baking soda in the warm water. Add to the batter and mix well. Spoon into 3 greased and floured 8-inch cake pans. Bake at 350 degrees for 25 minutes or until the layers test done. Remove to wire racks to cool. Spread the Boiled Icing between the layers and over the top and side of the cake. May bake in a lightly greased and floured 9x13-inch cake pan for 45 minutes or until cake tests done. Yield: 12 to 16 servings.

BOILED ICING

1/2	cup butter
1/2	cup margarine
2	cups sugar
1	cup evaporated milk
1	teaspoon vanilla extract

Melt the butter and margarine in a saucepan. Stir in the sugar and evaporated milk. Cook over low heat for 45 minutes, stirring occasionally. Remove from the heat and let stand until cool. Add the vanilla. Beat until thick and creamy and of the desired spreading consistency.

GARDEN PARTY CARROT CAKE WITH CREAM CHEESE FROSTING

This recipe is also called "Fourteen Karat Cake." It is a rich treat for your recipe collection.

2	cups flour
2	teaspoons baking powder
1½	teaspoons baking soda
1	teaspoon salt
2	teaspoons cinnamon
4	eggs
2	cups sugar
1½	cups vegetable oil
2	cups grated carrots
1	(8-ounce) can crushed pineapple, drained
½	cup chopped nuts
·	Cream Cheese Frosting

Sift the flour, baking powder, baking soda, salt and cinnamon together. Beat the eggs in a large bowl using a wire whisk. Add the sugar and vegetable oil and mix well. Stir in the flour mixture. Fold in the carrots, pineapple and nuts. Spoon into 3 greased and floured 9-inch cake pans. Bake at 350 degrees for 35 to 40 minutes or until the layers pull slightly from the side of the pans. Cool in the pans for 10 minutes. Invert onto wire racks to cool completely. Spread the Cream Cheese Frosting between the layers and over the top and side of the cake. May bake in a 10-inch tube pan for 50 minutes. Yield: 12 servings.

CREAM CHEESE FROSTING

½	cup butter or margarine, softened
8	ounces cream cheese, softened
1	teaspoon vanilla extract
1	(16-ounce) package confectioners' sugar

Beat the butter and cream cheese in a mixer bowl until smooth. Add the vanilla and mix well. Add the confectioners' sugar gradually, beating well after each addition.

FRESH COCONUT CAKE

Simply fabulous for any party. The cake would be a perfect wedding cake, but you may wish to use a different frosting.

1½	cups flour
2	teaspoons baking powder
½	cup butter, softened
1	cup sugar
2	egg yolks
½	cup milk
1	teaspoon vanilla extract
2	egg whites, stiffly beaten
·	Fluffy Coconut Frosting

Sift the flour and baking powder together 3 times. Cream the butter and sugar in a large mixer bowl until light and fluffy. Add the egg yolks and beat well. Add the sifted flour mixture and milk alternately, beating well after each addition and ending with the flour mixture. Beat in the vanilla. Stir in 1 heaping tablespoon of the stiffly beaten egg whites. Fold in the remaining stiffly beaten egg whites. Pour into a greased 9x13-inch cake pan. Bake at 350 degrees for 30 minutes or until the cake tests done. Cool on a wire rack. Invert onto a cake plate. Spread the Fluffy Coconut Frosting over the top and side of the cake. Pat the reserved coconut on the top and side of the cake. Cool the cake completely before serving. May use two 8x8-inch cake pans or two 9-inch cake pans. Yield: 15 servings.

FLUFFY COCONUT FROSTING

1	large coconut
1	cup sugar
¼	teaspoon cream of tartar
2	egg whites
½	teaspoon vanilla extract

Crack the coconut, reserving the liquid. Grate the coconut. Add enough water to the reserved coconut liquid to measure ⅓ cup. Combine with the sugar and cream of tartar in a saucepan. Cook over medium heat to 230 to 234 degrees on a candy thermometer, spun-thread stage; do not stir. Beat the egg whites in a mixer bowl until stiff peaks form. Add the sugar mixture gradually, beating constantly. Add the vanilla and beat well. Fold in ⅓ of the grated coconut, reserving the remaining coconut for the top and side of the cake. Continue to beat for a few minutes.

Cooke's son returned the ten-pound leather Bible to First Presbyterian Church in 1928, sixty-three years after it had been taken and just as the congregation was dedicating their new church building. As providence would have it, Lt. Cooke had unwittingly safeguarded the Bible that would have undoubtedly been destroyed in a devastating fire in the sanctuary on New Year's Eve, 1925.

HUMMINGBIRD CAKE

A time-tested blue-ribbon winner.

3	cups flour
1	teaspoon baking soda
1/2	teaspoon salt
2	cups sugar
1	teaspoon cinnamon
3	eggs, beaten
3/4	cup vegetable oil
1 1/2	teaspoons vanilla extract
1	(8-ounce) can crushed pineapple
1	cup chopped pecans
1 3/4	cups mashed bananas
·	Cream Cheese Frosting (page 152)
1/2	cup chopped pecans

Mix the flour, baking soda, salt, sugar and cinnamon in a large bowl. Add the eggs and vegetable oil, stirring just until the dry ingredients are moistened; do not beat. Stir in the vanilla, undrained pineapple, 1 cup pecans and bananas. Pour into 3 greased and floured 9-inch cake pans. Bake at 350 degrees for 23 to 28 minutes or until the layers test done. Cool in the pans for 10 minutes. Invert onto wire racks to cool completely. Spread Cream Cheese Frosting between the layers and over the top and side of the cake. Sprinkle the top with 1/2 cup chopped pecans. Yield: 12 to 16 servings.

ITALIAN CREAM CAKE

1	teaspoon baking soda
1	cup buttermilk
1/2	cup margarine, softened
1/2	cup shortening
2	cups sugar
5	egg yolks
2	cups sifted flour
1	teaspoon vanilla extract
5	egg whites, stiffly beaten
1	cup chopped pecans
1	(4-ounce) can flaked coconut
•	Cream Cheese Frosting (page 152)
1	cup finely chopped pecans

Dissolve the baking soda in the buttermilk. Let stand for a few minutes. Cream the margarine, shortening and sugar in a mixer bowl until light and fluffy. Add the egg yolks 1 at a time, beating well after each addition. Add the buttermilk mixture alternately with the flour, beating well after each addition. Stir in the vanilla. Fold in the stiffly beaten egg whites. Stir in 1 cup chopped pecans and coconut gently. Pour into 3 greased and floured 9-inch cake pans. Bake at 325 degrees for 25 minutes or until the cake tests done. Cool in the pans for a few minutes. Invert onto wire racks to cool completely. Spread Cream Cheese Frosting between the layers and over the top and side of the cake. Sprinkle the side of the cake with 1 cup finely chopped pecans. Yield: 12 to 16 servings.

CARAMEL NUT POUND CAKE

3	cups flour
1/2	teaspoon baking powder
1/2	teaspoon salt
1	cup butter, softened
1/2	cup shortening
1	(16-ounce) package light brown sugar
1	cup sugar
5	eggs
1	cup milk
1	tablespoon vanilla extract
1	cup chopped nuts

Mix the flour, baking powder and salt together. Cream the butter, shortening and brown sugar in a mixer bowl until light and fluffy. Add the sugar gradually, beating constantly. Add the eggs 1 at a time, beating well after each addition. Add the flour mixture alternately with the milk, beating well after each addition and ending with the flour. Stir in the vanilla and nuts. Pour into a greased and floured tube pan. Bake at 325 degrees for 1 1/2 hours or until the cake tests done. Cool in the pan for 15 minutes. Invert onto a wire rack to cool completely.
Yield: 20 servings.

SIX-FLAVOR POUND CAKE

A favorite Christmas cake recipe during the Depression, neighbors in the Piedmont Region of North Carolina, would share the flavorings used in the recipe to lower the expense of preparing the cake.

3	cups sugar
1	cup butter, softened
1/2	cup shortening
5	large eggs
1	teaspoon vanilla extract
1	teaspoon coconut extract
1	teaspoon almond extract
1	teaspoon lemon extract
1	teaspoon rum extract
1	teaspoon vanilla butternut extract
3	cups sifted flour
1/2	teaspoon baking powder
1	cup evaporated milk
•	Six-Flavor Glaze

Cream the sugar, butter and shortening at medium speed in a mixer bowl. Add the eggs 1 at a time, beating well after each addition. Add the flavorings 1 at a time, beating well after each addition. Mix the flour and baking powder together. Add to the creamed mixture alternately with the evaporated milk, beating at low speed after each addition. Pour into a greased and floured 10-inch tube pan. Bake at 300 degrees for 1 3/4 hours. Pierce the top of the hot cake with a wooden pick. Pour the Six-Flavor Glaze over the cake. Let stand for 15 to 20 minutes. Invert onto a cake plate. Let stand until cooled completely. Yield: 16 servings.

SIX-FLAVOR GLAZE

1	cup sugar
1/2	cup water
1/2	teaspoon each vanilla extract, coconut extract, almond extract, lemon extract, rum extract and vanilla butternut extract

Combine the sugar, water and flavorings in a small saucepan. Cook over low heat until the sugar dissolves, stirring constantly. Remove from the heat. Let stand until cool.

By 1953 he founded the University of North Carolina-Wilmington Department of Art and the state's reference collection of North Carolina Art and Artists. Artist, art historian, educator, advocate, and author, Howell received from Wake Forest University in 1975 an honorary doctorate of humanities. With his support, St. John's is the only museum dedicated to collecting and preserving three centuries of North Carolina art.

PUMPKIN CREAM CHEESE ROLL

3/4	cup flour
1	teaspoon baking soda
1/2	teaspoon salt
1	teaspoon ground cinnamon
1	teaspoon grated nutmeg
1	teaspoon ground ginger
1	teaspoon ground cloves
3	eggs
1	cup sugar
2/3	cup pumpkin purée
1	teaspoon lemon juice
1	cup chopped walnuts
·	Confectioners' sugar
·	Cream Cheese Filling

Whisk the flour, baking soda, salt, cinnamon, nutmeg, ginger and cloves together. Beat the eggs at high speed in a large mixer bowl. Add the sugar gradually, beating constantly for 5 minutes. Stir in the pumpkin and lemon juice. Add the flour mixture and mix well. Spoon into a 10x15-inch jelly roll pan lined with waxed paper. Sprinkle with the walnuts. Bake at 375 degrees for 15 minutes or until the top springs back when lightly touched. Loosen the edges with a knife and invert onto a towel sprinkled with confectioners' sugar. Remove the waxed paper. Roll up the cake in the towel, beginning with the short side. Let stand on a wire rack until cool. Unroll the cake and remove the towel. Spread Cream Cheese Filling to 1/2 inch from the edges of the cake and roll up. Place seam side down on a cake plate. Chill, covered, in the refrigerator until set. May freeze for up to 2 months.
Yield: 12 servings.

CREAM CHEESE FILLING

8	ounces cream cheese, softened
1/4	cup butter, softened
1/2	teaspoon vanilla extract
1	cup confectioners' sugar

Beat the cream cheese, butter and vanilla in a mixer bowl until light and fluffy. Add the confectioners' sugar and beat until smooth.

RED VELVET CAKE

2½   cups flour
1   teaspoon baking soda
1   teaspoon salt
1½   cups sugar
1   cup buttermilk
1¾   cups vegetable oil
2   eggs
1   teaspoon vanilla extract
1   teaspoon vinegar
¼   cup red food coloring
·   Cream Cheese Frosting (page 152)

Sift the flour, baking soda and salt together. Beat the sugar, buttermilk, vegetable oil and eggs in a large mixer bowl. Add the flour mixture and mix well. Stir in the vanilla, vinegar and food coloring. Pour into 3 greased and floured 8-inch cake pans. Bake at 350 degrees for 30 to 35 minutes or until the layers test done. Cool in the pans for a few minutes. Invert onto wire racks to cool completely. Spread Cream Cheese Frosting between the layers and over the top and side of the cake. Yield: 12 servings.

Her husband was a body servant for wealthy landowner Pembroke Jones; she was a domestic at the Jones' Airlie Estate. Inspired by her first vision on Good Friday in 1935, she began her artistic journey. In 1948 she became a gatekeeper at Airlie Gardens, often selling her drawings for fifty cents. The discovery of her art in 1962 led to exhibitions; however, she kept her job as gatekeeper until 1974 when her health failed. Minnie died in Wilmington at the age of ninety-five.

SUPER STRAWBERRY SHORTCAKE

2	cups flour
2	teaspoons baking powder
½	cup sugar
½	cup melted butter
⅔	cup milk
·	Whipped Almond Frosting
·	Sliced fresh strawberries
·	Sprigs of fresh mint

Sift the flour and baking powder into a bowl. Add the sugar and mix well. Blend in the melted butter. Stir in the milk. The mixture will not be smooth. Spoon the batter into a greased 9-inch cake pan or 8x8-inch cake pan. Bake at 450 degrees for 15 to 20 minutes or until the cake tests done. Cool in the pan for a few minutes. Invert onto a wire rack to cool completely. Cut the layer horizontally into halves. Place the bottom layer cut side up on a cake plate. Spread 1 cup of the Whipped Almond Frosting over the layer. Arrange sliced strawberries over the layer. Top with the remaining layer cut side down. Cover the top with 1 cup of the Whipped Almond Frosting. Arrange sliced strawberries over the top. Place a large dollop of Whipped Almond Frosting in the center. Garnish with sprigs of mint. Store in the refrigerator. Yield: 8 servings.

WHIPPED ALMOND FROSTING

¼	cup flour
1	cup milk
½	cup butter, softened
½	cup shortening
1	cup sugar
2	teaspoons almond extract

Combine the flour and milk in a saucepan. Cook until thickened, stirring constantly. Remove from the heat. Let stand until cooled. Beat the butter, shortening and sugar in a mixer bowl until smooth. Beat in the almond extract. Add the cooled flour mixture. Whip for 4 minutes.

PEANUT BRITTLE

Listed on the National Register of Historic Places is Wilmington's Poplar Grove Plantation. Prosperous before the Civil War, Poplar Grove survived the war's ravage and flourished with the cultivation of peanuts as its cash crop. The original house, destroyed by fire, was replaced by the 1850 Greek Revival house. Poplar Grove hosts special events and demonstrations and is a popular site for wedding parties.

1	cup sugar
1	cup raw peanuts
½	cup light corn syrup
⅛	teaspoon salt
1	teaspoon vanilla extract
1	tablespoon butter
1	teaspoon baking soda

Mix the sugar, peanuts, corn syrup and salt in a 9x13-inch microwave-safe dish. Microwave on High for 4 minutes. Stir well using a wooden spoon. Microwave for 4 minutes. Stir in the vanilla and butter. Microwave for 2 minutes. Stir in the baking soda. Pour onto a heated buttered baking sheet. Let stand until cool. Break into pieces. Do not substitute for the butter in this recipe. Yield: 1 pound.

SPECIAL BROWNIES

A little bite goes a long way.

2	ounces unsweetened chocolate
1/2	cup butter
1	cup sugar
2	eggs, beaten
1/2	cup flour
1/2	cup chopped pecans
•	Buttercream Frosting
2	ounces unsweetened chocolate
2	tablespoons butter

Combine 2 ounces unsweetened chocolate and 1/2 cup butter in a 4-cup microwave-safe bowl. Microwave on High until melted. Add the sugar, eggs and flour and mix well. Stir in the pecans. Spoon into a greased 9x13-inch glass baking dish. Bake at 350 degrees for 20 minutes or until the brownies pull away from the side of the dish. Let stand until cool. Spread Buttercream Frosting over the top. Chill in the refrigerator. Melt 2 ounces unsweetened chocolate and 2 tablespoons butter in a saucepan, stirring to mix well. Pour over the Buttercream Frosting, tilting the pan so the chocolate mixture will spread evenly. Let stand until cool. Cut into bite-size pieces. Yield: 9 to 10 dozen.

BUTTERCREAM FROSTING

1/4	cup butter, softened
2	cups confectioners' sugar
2	tablespoons milk
1/2	teaspoon vanilla extract

Beat the butter in a mixer bowl until fluffy. Add the confectioners' sugar, milk and vanilla and beat until smooth.

CHOCADAMIA COOKIES

1	cup rolled oats
1	cup flour, sifted
1/2	cup butter or margarine, softened
1/2	cup packed light brown sugar
1/4	cup sugar
1	egg
1	tablespoon water
1	teaspoon vanilla extract
1/2	teaspoon baking soda
1/8	teaspoon salt
8	ounces semisweet chocolate, cut into chunks
1 3/4	cups macadamia nuts or walnuts, coarsely chopped

Process the oats in a blender or food processor until finely ground. Combine the ground oats, flour, butter, brown sugar, sugar, egg, water, vanilla, baking soda and salt in a large mixer bowl. Beat at low speed until mixed, scraping the side of the bowl occasionally. Stir in the chocolate and macadamia nuts. Drop by rounded tablespoonfuls 2 inches apart on lightly greased cookie sheets. Bake at 350 degrees for 10 minutes or until light brown. Cool on the cookie sheets for 1 minute. Remove to wire racks to cool completely. Yield: 2 1/2 to 3 dozen.

Note: The dough may be easier to work with if chilled, rolled into small balls, placed on the cookie sheet and then flattened with a spatula.

Often included in Sports Hall of Fame exhibits are: Football's Roman Gabriel and Sonny Jurgensen, and the Harlem Globetrotters' Meadowlark Lemon, all native Wilmingtonians. Also included is World Tennis Champion Althea Gibson, who was victorious at U.S. Open and French Open Tournaments and won the women's singles title at Wimbledon in 1957 and 1958. A native New Yorker, she lived in Wilmington as a family member of her mentor, Dr. Hubert Eaton, a prominent local citizen and a national Junior Tennis Champion in 1934.

AUNT AMORET'S FIG COOKIES

For more than two hundred years, Anne Russell's family have always had fig trees on their property and have made ample use of them in season.

½	cup molasses
½	(16-ounce) package light brown sugar
4	eggs
1	cup (or more) flour
1	teaspoon baking soda
·	Ground cinnamon, nutmeg and cloves to taste
4	cups chopped fresh figs
1	cup pecan pieces

Combine the molasses, brown sugar and eggs in a mixer bowl and mix well. Add the flour, baking soda, cinnamon, nutmeg and cloves and mix well. Stir in the figs and pecans. The dough should be stiff; add additional flour if needed. Drop by spoonfuls onto greased cookie sheets. Bake at 350 degrees until light brown. Cool on wire racks. Yield: 2 to 3 dozen.

PECAN BARS

This recipe, similar to old-fashioned tea cakes, was submitted by a survivor of domestic violence. Domestic Violence Shelter and Services, Inc., was founded in 1986 through the consolidation of the community's two existing domestic violence programs. DVSS works towards the elimination of violence and oppression against women and their children and provides emergency and support services for victims and survivors of domestic violence.

2	eggs
1	cup sugar
⅔	cup melted butter
1	cup self-rising flour
2	teaspoons vanilla extract
2	cups chopped pecans

Beat the eggs, sugar and butter in a large mixer bowl. Add the flour and vanilla and mix well. Stir in the pecans. Spoon into an 8x11-inch nonstick baking pan. Bake at 350 degrees for 30 minutes. Let stand until cool. Cut into bars. Yield: 2 dozen.

RUGELACH

The oldest house of Jewish worship in North Carolina is in Wilmington. The Temple of Israel congregation was organized in 1872 and the synagogue was dedicated in 1876. This popular crescent-shaped cookie is traditionally served for Hanukkah. It is also great for gift-giving.

2	cups flour
1/4	teaspoon salt
1	cup unsalted butter, chilled, chopped
6	ounces cream cheese, chopped
1/3	cup sour cream
1/2	cup sugar
1	tablespoon cinnamon
1	cup finely chopped walnuts
1/2	cup chopped raisins (optional)

Combine the flour and salt in a bowl. Cut in the butter until crumbly. Add the cream cheese and sour cream and mix until the mixture holds together; the mixture will be crumbly. Shape into 4 equal-size disks. Wrap in plastic wrap. Chill for 1 to 2 hours or for up to 2 days. Mix the sugar and cinnamon in a bowl. Roll each disk into a 9-inch circle on a pastry board sprinkled with additional sugar, keeping the disks chilled until ready to use. Sprinkle each circle with the cinnamon-sugar, walnuts and raisins and press lightly into the dough. Cut each circle into 12 wedges. Roll up tightly from the outside edge to the point, enclosing the filling. Place on greased or parchment-lined cookie sheets. Chill for 20 minutes. Bake at 350 degrees for 15 to 20 minutes or until light golden brown. Cool partially on wire racks. Serve warm or store in an airtight container for up to 4 days. Yield: 4 dozen.

Note: May spread your favorite jam on the dough instead of using the cinnamon-sugar.

Television's Matlock series and films such as Sleeping with the Enemy, Firestarter, and Teenage Mutant Ninja Turtles are among those filmed in Wilmington. Many actors own homes and businesses locally; star-gazing has become a Wilmington pastime.

BLUEBERRY SOUR CREAM PIE

1	cup sour cream
3/4	cup sugar
2	tablespoons flour
1/4	teaspoon salt
1	egg, beaten
1	teaspoon vanilla extract
2½	cups fresh blueberries
1	unbaked (9-inch) pie shell
3	tablespoons flour
3	tablespoons butter, softened
3	tablespoons chopped pecans or walnuts

Combine the sour cream, sugar, 2 tablespoons flour, salt, egg and vanilla in a mixer bowl. Beat at medium speed for 5 minutes or until smooth. Fold in the blueberries. Pour into the pie shell. Bake at 400 degrees for 25 minutes. Combine 3 tablespoons flour, butter and pecans in a bowl and mix well. Sprinkle over the pie. Bake for 10 minutes. Let stand until cool. Chill, covered, until serving time. Yield: 6 to 8 servings.

At the mouth of the Cape Fear River is the island known as Bald Head. It's accessible only by boat, and transportation on the island is only by golf cart. It is both residential and resort in nature, and has a semi-tropical climate where certain plants co-exist that do not co-exist anywhere else. Its uniqueness doesn't stop with lush plant and animal life, some of which is threatened or endangered. Evidence shows the Indians also made annual excursions to the island for oysters and other shellfish. Pirates, privateers, river pirates, and commercial fishermen have made Bald Head their home.

▶

HEAVENLY LIME PIE

4	egg yolks
1/4	teaspoon salt
1/2	cup sugar
1/3	cup fresh lime juice
1	cup whipping cream, chilled
1	tablespoon grated lime peel
•	Meringue Shell

Beat the egg yolks in a mixer bowl until light and pale yellow. Stir in the salt, sugar and lime juice. Pour into a saucepan. Cook over medium heat for 5 minutes or until thickened, stirring constantly. Cool completely. Beat the whipping cream in a chilled bowl until stiff peaks form. Fold with the lime peel into the cooled mixture. Spoon into the Meringue Shell. Chill, covered, for 4 hours. Garnish with additional whipped cream and lime peel. May substitute lemon juice and peel for the lime. Yield: 8 servings.

MERINGUE SHELL

4	egg whites
1/4	teaspoon cream of tartar
1	cup sugar

Beat the egg whites and cream of tartar in a mixer bowl until foamy. Add the sugar 1 tablespoon at a time, beating for 10 minutes or until stiff and glossy. Pile into a buttered 9-inch pie plate, pushing up around the side to form a shell. Bake at 275 degrees for 1 hour or until firm and creamy white. Turn off the oven. Let stand in the oven for 1 hour; do not open the oven door. Remove from the oven and let stand on a wire rack until cooled completely.

There are legends and ghosts, as well as stories of gallant rescues of shipwrecked vessels, and picturesque "Old Baldy," the oldest lighthouse on the North Carolina coast, stands near the ramparts of an old Confederate fort.

DOUBLE-LAYERED PEACH PECAN PIE

A delectable dessert.

2	to 3 large peaches, peeled, seeded, chopped	1	teaspoon butter, softened
3	tablespoons sugar	1/2	teaspoon vanilla extract
•	Cornstarch (optional)	1/8	teaspoon salt
1/8	teaspoon cinnamon	1	teaspoon peach schnapps
1/8	teaspoon ground cloves	1/2	cup chopped pecans
1	medium egg, lightly beaten	2	(9-inch) deep-dish pie shells
3	tablespoons brown sugar	1/2	cup pecan halves
3	tablespoons dark corn syrup		

Cook the peaches and sugar in a saucepan over medium heat until soft and thick, stirring constantly. Add a small amount of cornstarch dissolved in a small amount of cold water if needed to thicken. Stir in the cinnamon and cloves. Let stand until cool. Combine the egg, brown sugar, corn syrup, butter, vanilla, salt and liqueur in a medium bowl and mix well. Sprinkle the chopped pecans in 1 of the pie shells. Add just enough of the egg mixture to coat the pecans. Remove the remaining pie shell from the foil pan and set inside the first pie shell, covering the pecan mixture. Press the bottom and side of the pie shells together and slightly build up the side. Trim and flute the edge using a knife tip. Cut several slits in the middle of the top pie shell. Add the pecan halves and peach mixture to the remaining egg mixture and mix well. Spoon into the top pie shell. Bake at 350 degrees for 45 minutes or until golden brown and a knife inserted in the center comes out clean. Yield: 8 servings.

SOUTHERN PECAN PIE

3	eggs, beaten	2	teaspoons vanilla extract
1	cup dark corn syrup	1/4	teaspoon salt
1/2	cup sugar	1	cup chopped pecans
2	tablespoons melted butter	1	unbaked (9-inch) pie shell

Combine the eggs, corn syrup, sugar, butter, vanilla and salt in a bowl and mix well. Stir in the pecans. Pour into the pie shell. Bake at 350 degrees for 50 minutes or until set. Yield: 6 servings.

Rum Chiffon Pie

1	tablespoon gelatin
1/4	cup cold water
1	cup milk
3	egg yolks
1/2	cup sugar
1	teaspoon vanilla extract
3	tablespoons rum
3	egg whites
1/4	teaspoon salt
1	baked (9-inch) pie shell
1	cup whipping cream
2	tablespoons confectioners' sugar
1/4	cup grated unsweetened chocolate

Soften the gelatin in the cold water. Scald the milk in a double boiler. Beat the egg yolks in a mixer bowl until light. Beat in the sugar gradually. Add the scalded milk and stir until the sugar is dissolved. Return to the double boiler. Cook over hot water until the mixture is the consistency of thick cream, stirring constantly. Remove from the heat. Stir in the softened gelatin and vanilla. Let stand until cool. Beat with a wire whisk until light. Add the rum and mix well. Beat the egg whites and salt in a mixer bowl until stiff peaks form. Fold into the custard. Pour into the pie shell. Chill in the refrigerator. Beat the whipping cream and confectioners' sugar in a mixer bowl until stiff peaks form. Spread over the pie, sealing to the edge. Sprinkle with the grated chocolate. Serve immediately. Yield: 8 servings.

No-Roll Pie Shell

1 1/2	cups flour
1 1/2	teaspoons sugar
1	teaspoon salt
1/2	cup vegetable oil
2	tablespoons cold milk

Mix the flour, sugar and salt together. Place in an ungreased pie plate. Whip the vegetable oil and milk in a bowl until cloudy in appearance. Add to the flour mixture and mix well. Press the dough over the bottom and up the side of the pie plate, trimming and fluting the edge. Prick with a fork. Bake at 400 degrees for 12 to 15 minutes or until golden brown. Yield: 1 pie shell.

Note: Omit the sugar when using the shell for a vegetable or meat pie.

The vision of her rubble on national television brought donations from all over the country to benefit the $1 million cost of restoration. Amazingly, the two-thousand-one-hundred-fifty-pound bell, which was almost two hundred years old, survived the fall relatively unscathed.

Cape Fear Cuisine

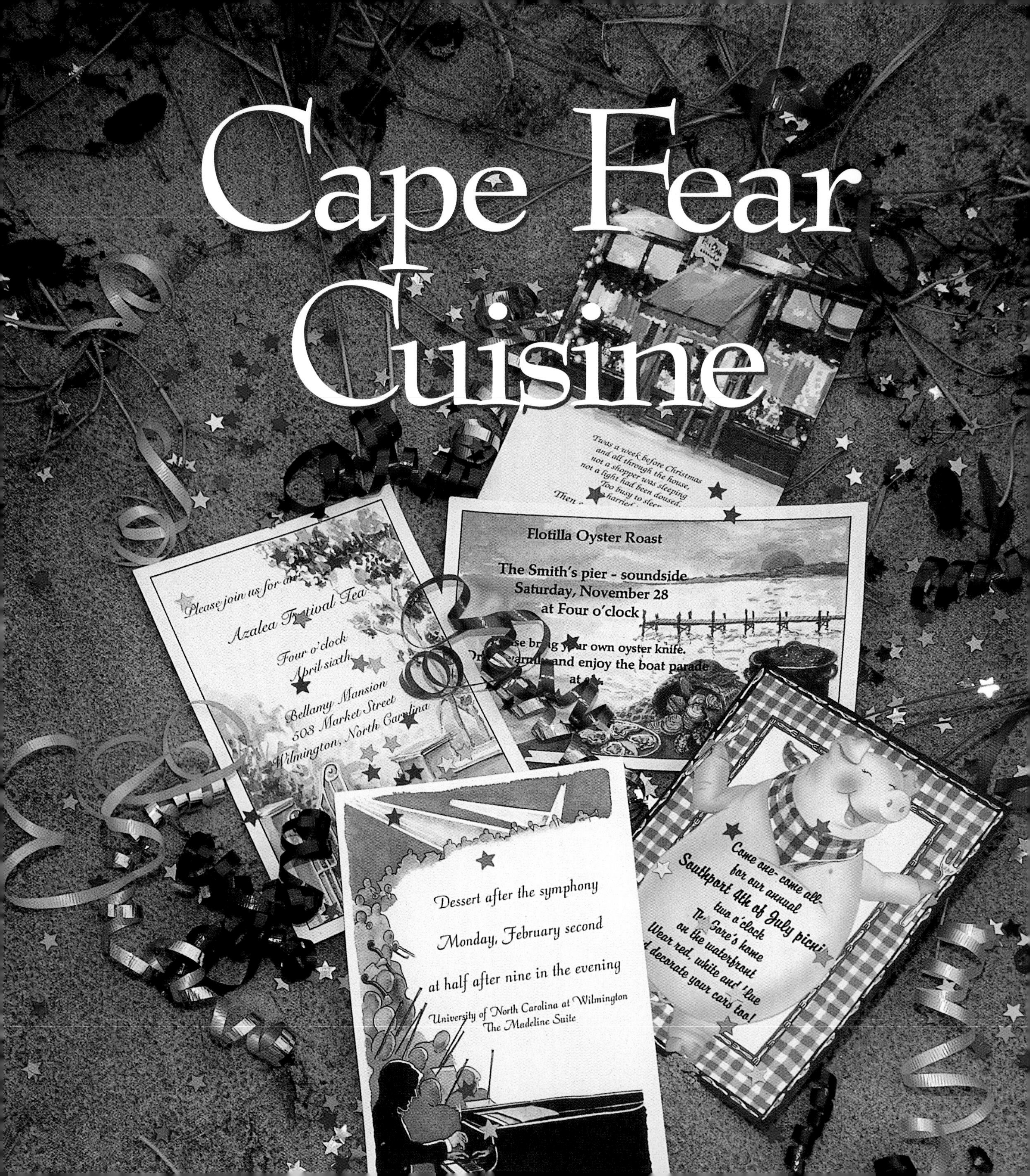

From cream puffs to good ol'

southern hush puppies,

join us in a tasteful journey of

some of the seasonal events

and festivals that dot the

calendar of Wilmington and

the Cape Fear coast.

SYMPHONY SWEETS

*A dessert lover's haven for an evening of indulgence at a party
after the symphony. These sweets are sure to tempt
all of your invited guests.*

Chocolate Nut Cakes

Chocolate Toffee Trifle

Kahlua Truffles

Praline Cheesecake

White Velvet with Raspberry Sauce

CHOCOLATE NUT CAKES

2¼ cups flour

1 teaspoon baking soda

1 teaspoon salt

1 cup shortening

2 cups sugar

5 eggs

3 ounces unsweetened chocolate, melted

1⅓ cups buttermilk

2 teaspoons vanilla extract

1 cup chopped walnuts

⅔ cup seedless raspberry jam, melted (optional)

· Chocolate Glaze (optional)

· Whipped cream (optional)

· Fresh raspberries (optional)

Mix the flour, baking soda and salt together. Beat the shortening in a mixer bowl until smooth and creamy. Add the sugar gradually, beating constantly at low speed until the mixture is light and fluffy. Add the eggs 1 at a time, beating well after each addition. Blend in the melted chocolate. Add the flour mixture alternately with the buttermilk, beating well after each addition and ending with the flour mixture. Stir in the vanilla and walnuts. Pour into 2 greased and floured 5x9-inch loaf pans. Bake at 350 degrees for 60 minutes or until the loaves test done. Cool in the pans for 10 minutes. Invert onto wire racks to cool completely. Place each loaf on a cake plate. Brush with the melted raspberry jam. Drizzle with the Chocolate Glaze. Pipe whipped cream down the center of each loaf and garnish with raspberries. Yield: 24 servings.

Note: May substitute sour milk for the buttermilk. To make sour milk, mix 4 teaspoons vinegar with enough milk to measure 1⅓ cups.

CHOCOLATE GLAZE

½ cup butter

8 ounces semisweet chocolate

Melt the butter and chocolate in a double boiler over hot water. Place the top of the double boiler over a bowl filled with ice. Stir until the mixture is slightly thickened. May microwave the butter and chocolate in a 4-cup microwave-safe bowl on High for 2 minutes and stir well. Microwave for 30 to 45 seconds longer or until the chocolate is melted and proceed as above.

CHOCOLATE TOFFEE TRIFLE

1	(2-layer) package devil's food cake mix
1	(4-ounce) package chocolate instant pudding mix
1½	cups milk
½	cup Kahlúa
6	(1-ounce) Heath bars, frozen
16	ounces whipped topping or sweetened whipped cream

Prepare and bake the cake using the package directions for a 9x13-inch cake. Let stand until cool. Cut the cake into 1-inch cubes. Combine the pudding mix, milk and Kahlúa in a bowl and mix well. Crush the candy in the wrappers with a hammer. Layer the cake cubes, pudding mixture, whipped topping and crushed candy ½ at a time in a trifle bowl. Chill, covered with plastic wrap, for 8 to 10 hours. Yield: 12 to 14 servings.

KAHLÚA TRUFFLES

1	cup whipping cream
6	tablespoons Kahlúa
18	ounces semisweet chocolate, melted
¾	cup butter, softened
·	Baking cocoa or chocolate sprinkles

Boil the whipping cream in a heavy saucepan until reduced to ¾ cup. Remove from the heat. Stir in the Kahlúa. Whisk in the melted chocolate and butter until smooth. Pour into shallow bowls. Chill in the refrigerator. Scoop into 1½-inch balls using a melon baller or teaspoon. Roll in baking cocoa or chocolate sprinkles. Place in foil candy cups. Store in the refrigerator. Yield: 24 servings.

Note: May pour the melted chocolate mixture into a candy mold sprayed with nonstick cooking spray, reserving some of the chocolate mixture for assembly. Chill for 1 hour or longer or until firm. Remove each ball of candy from the mold and spread with a small amount of reserved melted chocolate. Press the halves together. Chill in the refrigerator.

PRALINE CHEESECAKE

1½   cups graham cracker crumbs
½   cup melted butter or margarine
24   ounces cream cheese, softened
1¼   cups packed brown sugar
3   eggs
1   cup chopped pecans
2   tablespoons flour
1½   teaspoons vanilla extract
1   cup packed brown sugar
½   cup butter
·   Toasted pecan halves

Mix the graham cracker crumbs and ½ cup melted butter in a bowl. Press over the bottom of a 9-inch springform pan. Beat the cream cheese and 1¼ cups brown sugar in a mixer bowl until smooth. Beat in the eggs 1 at a time. Stir in the pecans, flour and vanilla. Pour into the prepared springform pan. Place on the middle oven rack. Place a baking pan filled with water on the rack underneath. Bake at 350 degrees for 50 to 55 minutes or until set. Let stand until cool. Combine 1 cup brown sugar and ½ cup butter in a saucepan. Cook over medium heat for 5 minutes or until smooth, stirring constantly. Pour over the cheesecake. Arrange toasted pecan halves on the top. Chill, covered, in the refrigerator.
Yield: 12 to 15 servings.

WHITE VELVET WITH RASPBERRY SAUCE

1½   teaspoons unflavored gelatin

2   tablespoons cold water

1   cup whipping cream

¼   cup sugar

1   cup sour cream

1   tablespoon fruit liqueur

·   Raspberry Sauce

Soften the gelatin in cold water in a small bowl. Heat the whipping cream over medium heat in a saucepan. Add the sugar and softened gelatin. Heat until dissolved, stirring constantly. Remove from the heat. Fold in the sour cream. Stir in the liqueur. Pour into 4 individual sherbet dishes, stemmed glasses or a decorative 2-cup mold. Chill, covered with plastic wrap, until set. Spoon Raspberry Sauce over the top just before serving. Yield: 4 servings.

Note: May substitute fresh fruit of choice for the Raspberry Sauce.

RASPBERRY SAUCE

1   (10-ounce) package frozen raspberries

¼   cup superfine sugar

2   tablespoons Grand Marnier

Thaw the raspberries and drain well. Combine the raspberries, sugar and Grand Marnier in a blender or food processor container. Process until puréed.

Note: May drizzle the sauce in a pattern on a dessert plate and arrange a slice of Chocolate Nut Cake (page 173) on the plate.

Azalea Festival Tea

The annual Azalea Festival is a social extravaganza that centers around the azalea flower. The city of Wilmington adorns itself in splendid natural regalia as the azalea blooms make their yearly spring visit, literally turning the city shades of pink, purple, and white. Southern heritage and genteel hospitality offer premier enjoyment for local natives and visitors alike as the celebration explodes with lots of food and fun.

Fruited Iced Tea

Cheese Straws

Mushroom Turnovers

Olive- and Pecan-Stuffed Cherry Tomatoes

Tea Party Sandwiches

Lace Cookies

Raspberry Swirl Cookies

Miniature Pecan Tarts

FRUITED ICED TEA

1	gallon water
7	tea bags
4	sprigs of fresh mint
·	Juice of 3 lemons
1	(6-ounce) can frozen orange juice concentrate
1/3	cup superfine sugar

Boil the water in a large saucepan. Add the tea bags and mint. Remove from the heat. Let steep for 15 minutes. Discard the tea bags and mint. Add the lemon juice, orange juice concentrate and sugar and mix well. Pour into a large pitcher. Chill until serving time. Serve over ice in glasses. Yield: 12 servings.

CHEESE STRAWS

1/2	cup butter, softened
1	pound sharp Cheddar cheese, grated
1 1/2	cups flour, sifted
1	teaspoon baking powder
1	teaspoon salt
1/4	to 1/2 teaspoon cayenne
1/4	teaspoon black pepper
1/4	clove of garlic, crushed

Beat the butter in a mixer bowl until creamy. Add the cheese, flour, baking powder, salt, cayenne, black pepper and garlic and knead until smooth. Brush a cookie press tube with additional flour. Fill the tube with the pastry. Pipe in 2-inch strips onto a nonstick baking sheet. Bake at 250 degrees for 30 to 40 minutes or until light brown. Yield: 7 to 8 dozen.

Variation: Shape the pastry into 1-inch balls and flatten with a fork. Top each with a pecan half. Bake as above.

MUSHROOM TURNOVERS

1/2	cup butter or margarine, softened
8	ounces cream cheese, softened
1 3/4	cups flour
8	ounces fresh mushrooms, minced
1	large onion, minced
3	tablespoons butter or margarine
1/2	cup sour cream
2	tablespoons flour
1	teaspoon salt
1/4	teaspoon thyme
1	large egg, lightly beaten

Beat 1/2 cup butter and cream cheese at medium speed in a mixer bowl until smooth. Add 1 3/4 cups flour gradually, beating well after each addition. Divide the dough into 2 equal portions. Shape each portion into a ball. Chill, covered, for 1 hour. Sauté the mushrooms and onion in 3 tablespoons melted butter in a large skillet until tender. Stir in the sour cream, 2 tablespoons flour, salt and thyme. Roll each dough portion 1/8 inch thick on a lightly floured surface. Cut into 2 1/2-inch circles. Place on greased baking sheets. Spoon 1 teaspoon of the mushroom mixture onto half of each circle. Moisten the edges with some of the beaten egg. Fold dough over the filling, pressing the edges with a fork to seal; prick the tops. Brush the turnovers with the remaining beaten egg. Bake at 450 degrees for 8 to 10 minutes or until golden brown. Yield: 3 1/2 dozen.

OLIVE- AND PECAN-STUFFED CHERRY TOMATOES

36   cherry tomatoes

2/3   cup toasted pecans, ground

1/3   cup finely chopped olives

1   to 2 tablespoons chopped cilantro

1   teaspoon finely shredded lemon peel

1/8   teaspoon pepper

Cut 1/4 inch from the top of each tomato. Remove the seeds and pulp to form a tomato shell using a 1/4-teaspoon measuring spoon. Mix the pecans, olives, cilantro, lemon peel and pepper in a small bowl. Spoon into the tomato shells. Chill, covered, until serving time. Yield: 3 dozen.

TEA PARTY SANDWICHES

11   ounces cream cheese, softened

1/4   cup milk

1   tablespoon Worcestershire sauce

12   ounces bacon, cooked, crumbled

1   loaf sliced white bread, crusts trimmed

1   loaf wheat bread, crusts trimmed

·   Pimento-stuffed olives, sliced

Beat the cream cheese, milk and Worcestershire sauce in a bowl until smooth. Stir in the bacon. Spread on the white bread slices; top with the wheat bread slices. Cut each sandwich into 3 equal portions. Top each with an olive slice. May make sandwiches 1 day in advance, covering with a damp paper towel and refrigerating until serving time. May include 1/4 cup each minced green bell pepper and grated onion in the cream cheese mixture. Yield: 5 1/2 dozen.

LACE COOKIES

½	cup flour
¼	teaspoon baking powder
½	cup sugar
½	cup rolled oats
2	tablespoons whipping cream
⅓	cup melted butter
2	tablespoons white corn syrup or maple syrup
1	teaspoon vanilla extract

Sift the flour, baking powder and sugar into a large bowl. Add the oats, whipping cream, butter, corn syrup and vanilla and mix well by hand. Drop by ½ teaspoonfuls onto a buttered cookie sheet, allowing 12 to 16 cookies per sheet. Bake at 375 degrees for 7 minutes or until light brown and nearly transparent. Cool for 1 minute on the cookie sheet. Remove to a wire rack covered with parchment paper or a paper towel to cool completely. May return to the oven and reheat for just a moment if the cookies cool and harden too quickly. Yield: 4 dozen 2-inch cookies.

Note: Lace cookies should be brittle. Test one or two before baking the whole batch. If any of the cookies crumble, they make wonderful topping for ice cream.

Variations: To make cornucopias, drop by teaspoonfuls onto a buttered cookie sheet, allowing 6 cookies per cookie sheet. Bake as above. Remove from the cookie sheet when firm enough and roll each cookie around the handle of a wooden spoon, forming cornucopias. Place seam side down on parchment paper to cool. Fill each cornucopia with Hard Sauce or whipped cream just before serving. To make Hard Sauce, mix ¾ cup butter, softened, 1½ cups confectioners' sugar and 2 tablespoons brandy or vanilla extract until smooth. Yield: 2 dozen cornucopias.

To make cookie baskets, remove hot cookies from the cookie sheet and place in small custard cups, shaping each to form a basket. Let stand until cool. Remove from the custard cups. Fill each basket with a scoop of your favorite ice cream just before serving.

RASPBERRY SWIRL COOKIES

A blue ribbon winner.

2	cups flour
1	teaspoon baking powder
1/4	teaspoon salt
1/2	cup butter or margarine, softened
1	cup sugar
1	egg
1	teaspoon vanilla extract
·	Raspberry Filling

Mix the flour, baking powder and salt together. Beat the butter in a mixer bowl until smooth and creamy. Add the sugar gradually, beating at medium speed until light and fluffy. Add the egg and vanilla and mix well. Add the flour mixture and beat well. Shape into a ball. Chill, wrapped in plastic wrap, for 2 hours. Roll into a 9x12-inch rectangle on floured waxed paper. Spread with Raspberry Filling to within 1/2 inch of the edges. Roll as for a jelly roll, beginning at the long end and peeling the waxed paper from the dough. Pinch the side seam to seal, leaving the ends open. Wrap in plastic wrap. Chill for 1 hour or until firm. Unwrap the roll. Cut into 1/4-inch slices. Place 2 inches apart on greased cookie sheets. Bake at 375 degrees for 8 to 10 minutes or just until the cookies begin to brown around the edges. Cool on wire racks. Yield: 3 1/2 dozen.

RASPBERRY FILLING

1/2	cup raspberry jam
1/2	cup flaked coconut
1/4	cup finely chopped walnuts

Combine the raspberry jam, coconut and walnuts in a bowl and mix well.

MINIATURE PECAN TARTS

    2   eggs, lightly beaten

    6   tablespoons melted butter

    1½   cups firmly packed dark or light brown sugar

    ¼   teaspoon salt

    2   teaspoons vanilla extract

    2   cups chopped pecans

    ·   Tart Shells

    ·   Confectioners' sugar (optional)

Combine the eggs, butter, brown sugar, salt and vanilla in a medium mixer bowl and beat well. Spoon 1 teaspoon of the pecans into each Tart Shell. Cover with 2 teaspoons of the filling. Bake at 325 degrees for 30 minutes. Cool on wire racks. Sprinkle with confectioners' sugar just before serving. Yield: 4 dozen.

Note: These may be frozen for later use.

TART SHELLS

    6   ounces cream cheese, softened

    1   cup butter, softened

    2   cups flour

Beat the cream cheese and butter in a mixer bowl until smooth and creamy. Add the flour and mix well. Chill, covered, for 2 hours. Shape the dough into forty-eight 1-inch balls. Place each ball in paper-lined 1¾-inch muffin cups. Shape to form a shell.

FOURTH OF JULY PICNIC

The official North Carolina Fourth of July Festival at Southport is the town's most celebrated event. The patriotic holiday is greeted with an elaborate parade; music, arts, crafts, and food complement the festival. The grand finale—magnificent fireworks shot from a barge anchored in the water—receives rounds of applause as the brilliant colors splash across the sky and create spectacular reflections.

Oven-Baked Spareribs with North Carolina Barbecue Sauce

Two-Bean Salad

Picnic Potato Salad

Company Deviled Eggs

Corn Bread Sticks

Blueberry Pie

Homemade Ice Cream

Oven-Baked Spareribs with North Carolina Barbecue Sauce

4	pounds pork spareribs
3	quarts water
1/2	cup North Carolina Barbecue Sauce
1/2	cup water
·	North Carolina Barbecue Sauce for basting
·	Salt and pepper to taste

Bring the spareribs and 3 quarts water to a boil in a 6-quart stockpot; drain. Place the spareribs in a large bowl. Pour 1/2 cup North Carolina Barbecue Sauce over the spareribs, covering all sides. Pour 1/2 cup water in an 11x15-inch baking dish. Add the spareribs. Let stand for 30 minutes. Bake at 300 degrees for 2 hours or until very tender and brown, basting occasionally with additional North Carolina Barbecue Sauce. Season with salt and pepper. Serve with North Carolina Barbecue Sauce. Yield: 4 servings.

North Carolina Barbecue Sauce

1	cup apple cider vinegar
1/2	to 3/4 cup water
2/3	cup minced onion
1	clove of garlic, crushed
1/2	teaspoon salt
1	teaspoon black pepper
1	to 2 teaspoons red pepper flakes
1	teaspoon sugar
1	bay leaf
2/3	teaspoon thyme
3	tablespoons peanut oil
2	to 3 teaspoons dry mustard
4	to 6 teaspoons cold water

Combine the vinegar, 1/2 to 3/4 cup water, onion, garlic, salt, black pepper, red pepper flakes, sugar, bay leaf, thyme and peanut oil in a small stainless steel or enamel saucepan. Bring to a boil and reduce the heat. Simmer for 5 minutes. Dissolve the dry mustard in 4 to 6 teaspoons cold water in a small bowl. Add enough of the hot vinegar sauce to make a thin liquid. Add to the hot vinegar sauce and mix well. Let stand until cool. Discard the bay leaf. Store in an airtight container in the refrigerator. Yield: 2 cups.

Two-Bean Salad

3	plum tomatoes
1	medium cucumber
1	(16-ounce) can Great Northern beans, rinsed, drained
1	(15-ounce) can red kidney beans, rinsed, drained
¼	onion, finely chopped
2	tablespoons dried parsley flakes
2	tablespoons white wine vinegar
1	tablespoon olive oil
½	teaspoon salt
¼	teaspoon pepper

Peel the tomatoes and remove the seeds. Chop the tomatoes. Peel the cucumber and remove the seeds. Chop the cucumber. Combine the tomatoes, cucumber, Great Northern beans, kidney beans, onion, parsley flakes, white wine vinegar, olive oil, salt and pepper in a bowl and mix well. Chill, covered, in the refrigerator until serving time. Yield: 8 servings.

PICNIC POTATO SALAD

4	bacon slices
8	potatoes, boiled, peeled, chopped
4	hard-cooked eggs, chopped
3/4	cup chopped celery
1/4	cup chopped green bell pepper
1/4	cup chopped green onions
1 1/2	tablespoons chopped parsley
2	dill gherkins, chopped
12	Spanish olives, chopped
2/3	cup mayonnaise
2	tablespoons prepared mustard
·	Salt and pepper to taste

Fry the bacon in a skillet until crisp; drain, reserving 2 tablespoons bacon drippings. Crumble the bacon and set aside. Combine the potatoes, eggs, celery, green pepper, green onions, parsley, dill gherkins and olives in a large bowl and toss to mix well. Add the mayonnaise, mustard, salt and pepper and mix well. Add the crumbled bacon and reserved bacon drippings and mix well. Chill, covered, for 1 hour or longer. Spoon into a serving bowl. Yield: 6 servings.

COMPANY DEVILED EGGS

12	medium hard-cooked eggs, cooled
1/4	cup mayonnaise
1/4	cup vinegar
2	tablespoons prepared mustard
1/4	teaspoon pepper
24	baby shrimp, cooked
24	capers
·	Paprika to taste

Cut the eggs into halves lengthwise. Remove the yolks to a medium mixer bowl, reserving the egg whites. Add the mayonnaise, vinegar, mustard and pepper and mix until smooth. Pipe into the egg whites. Top each with 1 shrimp and a caper. Sprinkle with paprika. Yield: 24 servings.

CORN BREAD STICKS

1	egg, beaten
1/4	cup vegetable oil
1 1/2	cups milk or buttermilk
2	cups self-rising cornmeal

Grease cast-iron corn stick molds with shortening. Place in a 450-degree oven. Combine the egg, vegetable oil and milk in a bowl and mix well. Stir in the cornmeal. Pour into the preheated molds. Bake for 15 minutes or until golden brown. Invert onto a wire rack. Serve hot. Yield: 8 servings.

Variation: Pour batter into a greased cast-iron skillet or muffin cups and bake for 20 to 25 minutes or until golden brown for corn bread or corn muffins.

BLUEBERRY PIE

A very pretty pie and delicious.

4	cups fresh blueberries
3/4	cup sugar
1/2	cup water
2	tablespoons cornstarch
1	baked (9-inch) pie shell
1	pint whipping cream
1	tablespoon Cointreau (optional)
1/4	cup slivered almonds (optional)

Combine 1 cup of the blueberries, sugar and 1/2 cup water in a saucepan. Bring to a boil over medium-low heat. Cook for 5 minutes or until the blueberries are soft. Pour into a blender container and process until puréed. Return to the saucepan. Dissolve the cornstarch in a small amount of cold water in a bowl. Add to the puréed mixture. Cook for 2 to 4 minutes or until thickened, stirring constantly. Remove from the heat and cool for a few minutes. Fold in the remaining blueberries. Pour into the cooled baked pie shell. Chill, covered, for several hours. Beat the whipping cream in a mixer bowl until soft peaks form. Fold in the Cointreau. Spread over the pie, sealing to the edge. Sprinkle with the almonds. Yield: 6 servings.

HOMEMADE ICE CREAM

Two old-fashioned ice cream stands at Southport and Oak Island serve a most delicious treat. As each churn is opened, a uniquely Southern tradition is passed to the next generation. Memories are shared of a slower time, when it was a great thrill to be given a turn hand-cranking the freezer while enjoying a summer day with family and friends.

3	eggs
1½	cups sugar
1	(14-ounce) can sweetened condensed milk
½	teaspoon vanilla extract
1½	cups chopped fresh peaches or strawberries (optional)
2½	quarts milk

Beat the eggs and sugar in a mixer bowl until well mixed. Add the sweetened condensed milk and vanilla, beating constantly. Pour into a chilled ice cream freezer container. Stir in the peaches or strawberries. Add milk to the fill line. Freeze using the manufacturer's directions. Cover the freezer with newspapers to keep cold. May make the ice cream base 1 day in advance and store in the refrigerator.
Yield: 16 to 20 servings.

Note: The ice cream should freeze in 20 to 30 minutes. If not, then the brine is not cold enough. Add more ice cream salt to make it colder. If the ice cream freezes too fast, it will be icy, grainy or hard. If the ice cream freezes around the edge of the container and not in the center, it is too cold and too much salt has been used.

FLOTILLA OYSTER ROAST

*Every year all sizes of sailing crafts adorn themselves with
twinkling lights, Christmas holly, and the occasional inflated Santa
for the Holiday Flotilla at Wrightsville Beach. The floating parade hails the
beginning of the yuletide season with a luminous display.*

Peppy Popcorn

Baked Bean Medley

Oyster Roast

Seafood Jambalaya

Cajun Spiced Corn on the Cob

Carolina Coleslaw with Celery Seed Dressing

Shrimp and Bow Tie Pasta Salad

Southern Hush Puppies

Lemon Chess Pie

PEPPY POPCORN

2½	teaspoons grated Parmesan cheese
1	teaspoon salt
¾	teaspoon chili powder
½	teaspoon onion powder
½	teaspoon garlic powder
½	teaspoon paprika
½	teaspoon ground thyme
15	cups popped popcorn

Combine the Parmesan cheese, salt, chili powder, onion powder, garlic powder, paprika and thyme in a bowl and mix well. Coat the popped popcorn lightly with butter-flavor nonstick cooking spray. Sprinkle ⅓ of the cheese mixture over the popped popcorn in a large bowl and toss to mix well. Repeat the procedure 2 more times. Serve immediately. Yield: 30 servings.

BAKED BEAN MEDLEY

12   slices bacon

2   cups chopped onions

2   cloves of garlic, minced

2   (16-ounce) cans butter beans, drained

2   (17-ounce) cans lima beans, drained

2   (15-ounce) cans red kidney beans, drained

2   (15-ounce) cans pork and beans, drained

1¼   cups catsup

¾   cup molasses

½   cup packed brown sugar

2   tablespoons Worcestershire sauce

2   tablespoons prepared mustard

½   teaspoon pepper

Cook the bacon in a skillet until crisp. Remove the bacon to paper towels to drain, reserving the bacon drippings. Add the onions and garlic to the reserved bacon drippings. Sauté until tender; drain. Crumble the bacon into a large bowl. Add the sautéed mixture, butter beans, lima beans, kidney beans and pork and beans and mix well. Stir in the catsup, molasses, brown sugar, Worcestershire sauce, mustard and pepper. Spoon into 2 lightly greased 2½-quart bean pots or baking dishes. Bake, covered, at 375 degrees for 1 hour. Yield: 16 to 20 servings.

OYSTER ROAST

The Cape Fear Indians are known to have eaten oysters in 1725 when they camped along the Lower Cape Fear coast. This recipe comes from Gibbs Willard, who says the tastiest oysters slept in the sound last night!

It is interesting to note that the table is made of a sheet of plywood on sawhorses. Until recent centuries no home had a separate dining room. Residents constructed a table by setting a board on sawhorses. Committees became known as boards from that custom of gathering at such a table. (The original word for table in English is "board.") The sideboard was often called the "groaning board," due to the amount of food to eat and the aftermath of eating too much.

Make a tabletop of plywood and have 2 holes cut about a foot square. Set the tops on sawhorses and place baskets under each hole. When you open your own oyster, just drop the empty shell through the hole into the basket.

- 1   bushel oysters
- 1   metal box, or sheet of metal
- ·   Burlap bags
- 1   roaring fire under the metal

Place the oysters on top of the metal sheet and cover with wet burlap bags. Cook until the oysters open up and dry out a little—they will look lacy and frilly around the edges. Serve in a large aluminum dishpan, which helps to keep the oysters warm. Let everyone open his own oyster. At each place you will need a small bowl, heavy knife, a fork, and a small terry cloth towel. Offer hot pepper vinegar, pickle relish, catsup, and melted butter. Each guest concocts his own dip.

Roast 1 bushel of oysters at a time, keeping them cooking until everyone is fed.

May also steam oysters on top of the kitchen stove by placing them on a wire rack in a regular large roaster with a little water in the bottom or in a clam steamer. It's hard on the kitchen, but fine for a few people.

Yield: enough for 5 average appetites.

SEAFOOD JAMBALAYA

1	pound bacon
1	pound smoked sausage, thinly sliced
1	green bell pepper, chopped
1	yellow onion, chopped
2	cloves of garlic, chopped
1	cup chopped fresh parsley
1½	cups chopped celery
2	(16-ounce) cans tomatoes, chopped
1	cup chopped green onions
2	cups water
1½	teaspoons thyme
2	bay leaves
2	teaspoons oregano
2	tablespoons Tabasco sauce
½	teaspoon salt (optional)
1	tablespoon black pepper
2	fresh jalapeños, seeded, chopped
1	teaspoon cayenne, or to taste
½	teaspoon chili powder
½	teaspoon garlic powder
2	cups long grain rice, rinsed
3	pounds seafood, such as shrimp, scallops and cubed fish

Brown the bacon in a 4-quart stockpot; drain. Crumble the bacon and set aside. Brown the smoked sausage in the stockpot. Remove the smoked sausage and set aside. Add the green pepper, onion, garlic, parsley and celery to the stockpot. Sauté until tender. Stir in the undrained tomatoes, green onions and 2 cups water. Add the thyme, bay leaves, oregano, Tabasco sauce, salt, black pepper, jalapeños, cayenne, chili powder and garlic powder and mix well. Stir in the smoked sausage and crumbled bacon. Simmer, covered, for 15 minutes, stirring occasionally. Add the rice. Reduce the heat. Cook, covered, for 20 minutes or until most of the liquid has been absorbed by the rice. Add the seafood. Cook until the rice is tender and the seafood is cooked through. Remove the bay leaves. Serve with additional Tabasco sauce. Yield: 10 to 12 servings.

Note: May use such fish as grouper, redfish or mahimahi.

CAJUN SPICED CORN ON THE COB

Here's a recipe that adds a little zing to plain corn on the cob.

20	ears of fresh corn
2	cups butter, melted
1	tablespoon kosher salt
1/2	tablespoon garlic powder
1/2	tablespoon cayenne
3/4	teaspoon white pepper
3/4	teaspoon black pepper
3/4	teaspoon basil
3/4	teaspoon thyme
1/2	teaspoon (scant) oregano
·	Chopped parsley to taste

Shuck the corn and remove the silk. Cut the ears of corn into halves. Fill an 8-quart stockpot 3/4 full of water. Add the corn. Bring to a boil. Boil for 30 to 40 minutes or until the corn is tender; drain. Pour the butter over the corn in the stockpot. Combine the kosher salt, garlic powder, cayenne, white pepper, black pepper, basil, thyme and oregano in a sealable plastic bag and shake well. Add 2 to 3 tablespoons of the mixture to the corn, turning the corn to coat well. Reserve the remaining spice mix for another purpose. Place the corn in a large serving bowl. Sprinkle with parsley. Yield: 20 to 25 servings.

Carolina Coleslaw with Celery Seed Dressing

1	medium head cabbage
1/3	cup cider vinegar
2	eggs
1 1/2	teaspoons dry mustard
3	tablespoons sugar
1/2	teaspoon salt
3/4	cup whipping cream
1	tablespoon butter or margarine
1 1/2	teaspoons celery seeds

Remove the core from the cabbage and remove the outer leaves. Cut the cabbage into quarters. Cut each quarter into paper-thin slices and place in a large bowl. Bring the vinegar to a boil in a small saucepan. Beat the eggs lightly in a double boiler. Stir in the dry mustard, sugar and salt. Beat in the whipping cream. Add the boiling vinegar in a fine stream to the egg mixture, stirring constantly. Heat over simmering water for 3 to 5 minutes or until thickened, stirring constantly. Remove from the heat. Stir in the butter and celery seeds. Pour over the cabbage and toss to mix well. Chill, covered, for 2 to 3 hours. Toss well just before serving. Yield: 6 servings.

SHRIMP AND BOW TIE PASTA SALAD

3	(16-ounce) packages bow tie pasta
3	pounds (35- to 40-count) shrimp
1	bunch broccoli, cut into small pieces
1	head cauliflower, cut into small pieces
3	carrots, peeled, chopped
1	red onion, chopped
1	bunch green onions, chopped
3	cups mayonnaise
2	cups red wine vinegar
1¾	cups sugar
2	tablespoons garlic powder
1	tablespoon basil
1	tablespoon salt
1	tablespoon pepper
·	Chopped parsley to taste
·	Grated Parmesan cheese to taste

Cook the pasta in water to cover in a 6-quart stockpot for 10 to 12 minutes or until tender. Drain and rinse with cold water. Drain and set aside. Peel and devein the shrimp. Place in a large stockpot of boiling water. Cook for 3 to 5 minutes or until the shrimp turn pink. Rinse with cold water until cool. Combine the pasta, shrimp, broccoli, cauliflower, carrots, red onion and green onions in a large bowl and toss to mix well. Combine the mayonnaise, vinegar, sugar, garlic powder, basil, salt and pepper in a bowl and mix well. Add to the pasta mixture and toss to mix well. Spoon into a large serving bowl. Sprinkle with chopped parsley and Parmesan cheese. Yield: 20 to 25 servings.

SOUTHERN HUSH PUPPIES

¾	cup cornmeal
¼	cup flour
2	teaspoons baking powder
½	teaspoon salt
½	teaspoon garlic powder
¼	teaspoon cayenne
1	egg
½	cup (or more) buttermilk
·	Vegetable oil for deep-frying

Mix the cornmeal, flour, baking powder, salt, garlic powder and cayenne in a bowl. Add the egg and mix well. Stir in enough buttermilk to form a batter that can be molded by a spoon. Pour enough vegetable oil into a deep fryer to cover the hush puppies by 3 to 4 inches. Heat the vegetable oil to 375 degrees. Drop the batter by tablespoonfuls into the hot vegetable oil. Deep-fry for 3 to 5 minutes or until golden brown. Drain on paper towels. Serve hot. Yield: 20 servings.

LEMON CHESS PIE

6	egg yolks
1	cup sugar
1	cup whipping cream
2	teaspoons cornmeal
¼	cup fresh lemon juice
½	cup melted butter
1½	tablespoons flour
1	unbaked (10-inch) pie shell

Beat the egg yolks and sugar in a mixer bowl until thick and pale yellow. Add the whipping cream, cornmeal and lemon juice and mix well. Stir in the butter and flour. Spoon into the pie shell. Bake at 300 degrees for 30 minutes or until the center is set. Cool on a wire rack. Chill, covered, until serving time. Yield: 8 servings.

CHRISTMAS BY CANDLELIGHT

*The grand historic homes and churches of Wilmington are festooned with
the finest holiday decorations in time for the Old Wilmington by
Candlelight Tour benefiting the Lower Cape Fear Historical Society. The clip-clop
of horse drawn carriages and the songs of carolers on Victorian porches beckon
strolling visitors to enter an era where time seems to stand still.*

Holiday Eggnog

Christmas Wreath Soup

Beef Tenderloin

Cheese Soufflé

Company Peas

Mandarin Orange and Romaine Toss

Buttermilk Rolls

Christmas Cake

HOLIDAY EGGNOG

  4   egg yolks
  1   cup plus 2 tablespoons confectioners' sugar
  1 1/3   cups apple brandy
  2 2/3   cups whipping cream
  1 1/3   cups milk
  ·   Ground nutmeg to taste

Beat the egg yolks in a mixer bowl until light. Add the confectioners' sugar, brandy, whipping cream and milk 1 at a time, beating well after each addition. Pour into a punch bowl. Sprinkle with nutmeg. Yield: 1 2/3 quarts.

Variation: Whip 2 egg whites in a mixer bowl until stiff peaks form. Fold into the eggnog.

Note: The quantity of servings may be changed by increasing the ingredients by half or doubling them. To avoid raw eggs that may carry salmonella, use an equivalent amount of pasteurized egg substitute.

CHRISTMAS WREATH SOUP

  3   cups vegetable juice cocktail
  2   cups chicken stock or canned chicken broth
  2   tablespoons light brown sugar
  2   tablespoons sherry
  2   tablespoons butter
  2   tablespoons finely chopped parsley

Combine the vegetable juice cocktail, chicken stock, brown sugar and sherry in a double boiler. Heat over simmering water almost to the boiling point. Stir in the butter. Ladle into warm soup bowls. Top each serving with parsley sprinkled in the shape of a wreath. Yield: 6 servings.

Note: The quantity of servings may be changed by increasing the ingredients by half or doubling them.

BEEF TENDERLOIN

1	cup port
1	cup soy sauce
½	cup olive oil
1	teaspoon pepper
1	teaspoon thyme
½	teaspoon hot sauce
4	cloves of garlic, crushed
1	bay leaf
1	(5- to 6-pound) beef tenderloin

Combine the wine, soy sauce, olive oil, pepper, thyme and hot sauce in a bowl and mix well. Stir in the garlic and bay leaf. Place the tenderloin in a large plastic container with an airtight cover. Pour the wine mixture over the tenderloin. Marinate, tightly covered, for 8 hours, turning occasionally. Drain, reserving the marinade. Bring the reserved marinade to a boil in a saucepan. Boil for several minutes and remove from the heat. Place the tenderloin on a rack in a broiler pan. Insert a meat thermometer in the thickest portion, making sure it does not touch any fat. Bake at 425 degrees for 60 minutes or until the meat thermometer reaches 140 degrees for rare, 150 degrees for medium-rare or 160 degrees for medium, basting occasionally with the heated marinade. Yield: 10 to 12 servings.

CHEESE SOUFFLÉ

12	slices white bread, crusts trimmed
8	ounces sharp Cheddar cheese, grated (2½ cups)
2⅔	cups milk
4	eggs, lightly beaten
1	teaspoon salt, or to taste
·	Pepper to taste

Cut the bread slices into halves. Layer the bread and cheese ½ at a time in a buttered 2-quart or 9x13-inch baking dish. Pour a mixture of the milk, eggs, salt and pepper over the layers. Chill, covered, for 24 hours. Let stand at room temperature for 1 hour. Bake, uncovered, at 350 degrees for 45 to 60 minutes or until light brown and puffed. Yield: 8 to 10 servings.

COMPANY PEAS

6	tablespoons butter
2/3	cup chopped onion
3	cups thinly sliced celery
3	or 4 (10-ounce) packages frozen green peas
1/4	cup (or more) hot water
1½	teaspoons salt
·	Pepper to taste
·	Thyme to taste
1	teaspoon Worcestershire sauce
2	tablespoons chopped fresh parsley

Melt the butter in a sauté pan. Add the onion and celery. Sauté for 5 minutes or until golden brown. Add the peas, hot water, salt, pepper and thyme. Simmer, covered, for 8 minutes or until the peas are tender. Do not overcook. Add the Worcestershire sauce and parsley and mix lightly. Yield: 8 to 10 servings.

MANDARIN ORANGE AND ROMAINE TOSS

¼	cup vegetable oil
2	tablespoons sugar
2	tablespoons vinegar
1	tablespoon chopped fresh parsley
½	teaspoon salt
⅛	teaspoon pepper
⅛	teaspoon Tabasco sauce
¼	cup sliced almonds
4	teaspoons sugar
¼	head iceberg lettuce
¼	head romaine
2	ribs celery, chopped
2	green onions, chopped
1	(10-ounce) can mandarin oranges, drained

Combine the vegetable oil, 2 tablespoons sugar, vinegar, parsley, salt, pepper and Tabasco sauce in a jar with a lid. Cover with the lid and shake to mix well. Chill in the refrigerator. Combine the almonds and 4 teaspoons sugar in a skillet. Cook over low heat until the sugar dissolves and coats the almonds, stirring constantly. Let stand until cool and break apart. Combine the iceberg lettuce, romaine, celery and green onions in a large salad bowl and toss to mix well. Add the dressing and toss to mix well. Arrange the oranges over the top. Sprinkle with the sugared almonds. Yield: 6 to 8 servings.

Note: The quantity of servings may be changed by increasing the ingredients by half or doubling them.

BUTTERMILK ROLLS

4	to 4½ cups flour
½	teaspoon baking soda
½	teaspoon salt
2	envelopes dry yeast
¼	cup lukewarm water
1½	cups lukewarm buttermilk
3	tablespoons sugar
½	cup vegetable oil

Mix 4 cups of the flour, baking soda and salt together. Dissolve the yeast in the lukewarm water in a bowl. Add the buttermilk, sugar and vegetable oil. Add the flour mixture and mix until smooth. Stir in enough of the remaining flour to make a soft dough. Cover and let stand for 10 minutes. Roll the dough into a circle on a lightly floured surface. Cut into circles with a biscuit cutter. Fold each circle in half and place on a nonstick baking sheet. Cover with a cloth. Let rise for 30 minutes. Bake at 400 degrees for 15 to 20 minutes or until light brown.
Yield: 3½ to 4 dozen.

CHRISTMAS CAKE

2	cups flour
3	cups sugar
2	teaspoons baking soda
2	eggs, beaten
2	cups crushed pineapple
½	cup butter or margarine
1	(5-ounce) can evaporated milk
1	(7-ounce) can shredded coconut
1	teaspoon vanilla extract
1	cup chopped nuts

Sift the flour, sugar and baking soda into a large mixer bowl. Add the eggs and pineapple and mix well. Spoon into a greased 9x13-inch cake pan. Bake at 350 degrees for 30 minutes. Combine the butter and evaporated milk in a saucepan. Cook over low heat until the butter melts. Cook for 2 minutes longer and remove from the heat. Stir in the coconut, vanilla and nuts. Spread over the hot cake.
Yield: 20 servings.

Toast
Of The
Coast

In Wilmington, restaurants are a wonderful way to sample the variety of foods of the Lower Cape Fear. The city's growth has brought about many distinctive restaurants with unique atmospheres and flavorful food choices. Sample their recipes at home or out; they're a sure culinary success. Wherever you choose to entertain, at home or at a restaurant, it is your personal touches that may cause the first gathering to become a tradition. We toast you, the shining star, who brings friends and family together in laughter and sharing.

Restaurant:
Blockade Runner Resort Hotel
and Conference Center

Owner:
Four Seasons Management

ROASTED RACK OF LAMB WITH MUSTARD HERB CRUMBS

- ·   Vegetable oil
- 2   Frenched racks of lamb
- ·   Kosher salt to taste
- ·   Freshly ground black pepper to taste
- ·   Dijon mustard
- ·   Fresh chopped rosemary, sage and parsley to taste
- ·   Fresh bread crumbs

Heat a small amount of vegetable oil in a roasting pan. Season the lamb with kosher salt and pepper. Sear the lamb on all sides in the preheated vegetable oil. Bake at 375 degrees for 10 minutes. Remove from the oven. Brush with Dijon mustard. Coat the lamb with a mixture of chopped fresh herbs and bread crumbs. Bake for 5 minutes or until the bread crumbs are light brown. Remove from the oven and let stand for 15 minutes. Carve and serve with rosemary au jus and/or mint jelly. Yield: 16 servings.

BRONZED SALMON AND SHRIMP ON CAROLINA BABY GREENS WITH ZINFANDEL VINAIGRETTE

1½   pounds salmon fillet, skinned

12   (31- to 35-count) shrimp, peeled, deveined

·   Cajun blackening spice to taste

·   Olive oil

4   cups mixed baby greens

·   Zinfandel Vinaigrette

Cut the salmon into four 6-ounce portions. Dredge the salmon and shrimp in the Cajun blackening spice. Heat some olive oil in a large sauté pan. Add the salmon. Sear on both sides until bronzed. Remove and place in a baking pan. Bake at 350 degrees for 4 to 5 minutes or until the salmon flakes easily. Sauté the shrimp in some olive oil in a sauté pan until the shrimp turn pink. Remove from the pan and keep warm. Place 1 cup of the greens on each serving plate. Arrange 1 salmon fillet and 3 shrimp on the bed of greens. Drizzle with Zinfandel Vinaigrette. Yield: 4 servings.

ZINFANDEL VINAIGRETTE

¼   cup olive oil

¼   cup vegetable oil

2   tablespoons Zinfandel

2   tablespoons red wine vinegar

1   tablespoon minced shallots

1   teaspoon Dijon mustard

1   teaspoon sugar

¼   teaspoon salt

⅛   teaspoon pepper

Combine the olive oil, vegetable oil, Zinfandel, red wine vinegar, shallots, Dijon mustard, sugar, salt and pepper in a bowl and blend well. May store in the refrigerator for up to 1 week.

Restaurant:
Bocci

Chef:
Julian L. Harris

Owner:
Vance Donkle

Restaurant:
Brenner–An American Bistro

Chef:
Todd Brenner

Owners:
Todd and Sharon Brenner

MARINATED GROUPER WITH FRUIT SALSA

½	cup lime juice
¼	cup tequila
2	tablespoons chopped cilantro
1	medium shallot, chopped
1	clove of garlic, chopped
4	grouper fillets
·	Fruit Salsa

Mix the lime juice, tequila, cilantro, shallot and garlic in a small bowl. Let stand at room temperature to enhance the flavors. Brush the marinade on the fish shortly before grilling or broiling. Place on a grill rack. Grill until the fish flakes easily. Place on individual serving plates and spoon Fruit Salsa over the top. Yield: 4 servings.

Note: Alcohol that is left too long on fish and shellfish will work as a cooking agent.

FRUIT SALSA

½	fresh pineapple, finely chopped
½	cup finely chopped strawberries
¼	cup finely chopped kiwifruit
1	medium shallot or green onion, chopped
·	Cilantro to taste
·	Juice of 1 lime or lemon
·	Salt to taste
2	tablespoons chopped jalapeño

Mix the pineapple, strawberries, kiwifruit, shallot, cilantro, lime juice, salt and jalapeño in a bowl. May use any fruit in season in this recipe.

PEPPER BAKED SALMON WITH COUNTRY HAM AND OYSTER SAUCE

1/4	cup ground mixed white and black peppercorns
1	tablespoon kosher salt
1	tablespoon granulated garlic
1	tablespoon lemon pepper
4	(8-ounce) salmon fillets
8	ounces center-cut country ham
·	Oyster Sauce
·	Sprigs of fresh parsley

Mix the ground peppercorns, kosher salt, garlic and lemon pepper in a small bowl. Sprinkle over the salmon in a nonstick baking dish. Bake at 350 degrees for 15 to 20 minutes or until the salmon flakes easily. Cut the ham into 1/4-inch squares. Sauté the ham in a medium skillet over medium heat for 4 to 5 minutes or until cooked through. Place the salmon on individual serving plates. Spoon Oyster Sauce over the salmon and top with ham squares. Garnish with fresh parsley sprigs. Yield: 4 servings.

Note: Serve over grits for a real southern flavor.

OYSTER SAUCE

1	pint shucked oysters
1/2	cup butter
1	cup whipping cream
·	Salt and pepper to taste
2	tablespoons cornstarch
2	tablespoons water

Drain the oysters, reserving the liquid. Strain 1/2 of the reserved liquid. Combine the oysters, butter and all the liquid in a saucepan. Cook over medium-high heat for 12 minutes. Add the whipping cream. Bring to a slow boil and remove from the heat. Season with salt and pepper to taste. Add a mixture of cornstarch and water gradually, stirring constantly until thick.

Restaurant:
The Bridge Tender

Chef:
Fred Shaw

Owner:
Hanover Seafood Partners

Restaurant:
Caffé Phoenix

Chef:
Nancy Kaiser Bostian

Owners:
Deborah and Michael Caliva

Horseradish Encrusted Salmon over Garlic Mashed Potatoes with Dill Sour Cream Sauce

1	cup prepared horseradish	1/4	cup butter
1	cup country-style Dijon mustard	·	Garlic Mashed Potatoes
		·	Dill Sour Cream Sauce
1/2	cup fresh bread crumbs	·	Lemon slices
1	tablespoon thyme	·	Pink peppercorns
4	(7-ounce) salmon fillets	·	Fresh sprigs of dill
1	egg, beaten		

Combine the horseradish, Dijon mustard, bread crumbs and thyme in a bowl and mix well. Brush the top of each fillet with the beaten egg. Coat the top with the horseradish mixture. Melt the butter in a skillet until smoking. Add the salmon coated side down and sear until brown. Turn over the salmon and sear for a few seconds. Remove from the heat. Place in a nonstick baking pan. Bake at 400 degrees until the salmon flakes easily. Make a bed of Garlic Mashed Potatoes in the center of each plate. Place the salmon on top and drizzle with Dill Sour Cream Sauce. Garnish with lemon slices, pink peppercorns and fresh sprigs of dill.
Yield: 4 servings.

Garlic Mashed Potatoes

15	new potatoes	1	cup milk or whipping cream
·	Salt to taste		
1/4	cup butter, softened	·	Freshly ground pepper to taste
4	to 6 cloves of garlic, minced		

Cook the unpeeled potatoes in salted boiling water until tender. Drain and let the potatoes stand for 2 to 3 minutes to fluff. Mash the hot potatoes. Add the butter, garlic, milk, salt and pepper to taste and mix well.

Dill Sour Cream Sauce

1/2	cup chopped fresh dill	1/2	cup sour cream
1	cup white wine	·	Salt and freshly ground pepper to taste
1/4	cup lemon juice		
2	cups whipping cream		

Cook the dill, wine and lemon juice in a saucepan until reduced by half. Add the whipping cream. Simmer until thickened, stirring constantly. Whisk in the sour cream, salt and pepper.

CHICKEN CAPE FEAR

Restaurant:
Cape Fear Country Club

4	(4-ounce) boneless skinless chicken breasts
2	tablespoons flour
1/4	cup olive oil
8	ounces small shrimp
2	ounces prosciutto, chopped
6	medium mushrooms, sliced
2	green onions
1/2	cup white wine
•	Cream Sauce

Sprinkle the chicken with the flour. Sauté in the olive oil in a sauté pan for 2 to 3 minutes on each side. Remove from the pan and keep warm. Add the shrimp, prosciutto, mushrooms and green onions to the pan. Sauté for 1 minute. Add the wine. Cook until the liquid is reduced by half. Return the chicken to the pan. Strain the Cream Sauce over the chicken. Reduce the heat. Simmer for 5 minutes or until the chicken is cooked through. Serve over hot cooked pasta or rice. Yield: 4 servings.

CREAM SAUCE

1	tablespoon margarine
1	tablespoon flour
1 1/4	cups milk
1/8	teaspoon salt
1/8	teaspoon white pepper

Melt the margarine in a small saucepan. Stir in the flour to make a roux. Whisk in the milk. Simmer until thickened, whisking constantly. Season with salt and white pepper. Keep warm.

CAROLINA'S SHRIMP AND GRITS

1	tablespoon butter
1	ounce sliced yellow onion
1	ounce thinly sliced prosciutto
1	tablespoon white wine
4	(16- to 20-count) shrimp
½	cup whipping cream
2	tablespoons grated Parmesan cheese
1	(2-ounce) Grit Cake
⅛	teaspoon chopped fresh parsley

Melt the butter in a sauté pan over high heat. Add the onion and prosciutto. Sauté until light brown. Add the wine, stirring to deglaze the pan. Add the shrimp. Cook until the wine is reduced. Add the whipping cream and Parmesan cheese. Cook until thickened, stirring constantly and being careful to not overcook the shrimp. Spoon over the Grit Cake. Sprinkle with the parsley. Yield: 1 serving.

Note: To prepare Grit Cakes, cook grits using the package directions. Pour into a greased pan. Chill until firm. Cut into desired shapes.

Restaurant:
Carolina's Food and Drink

Chef:
Mark Lawson

Owners:
Ann Tobin and Joe Gondek

Buffalo Chicken Salad with Bleu Cheese Buttermilk Dressing

1 1/2   tablespoons olive oil
2   tablespoons hot sauce
1   tablespoon paprika
6   (4-ounce) skinless boneless chicken breast halves
1   large carrot
1   rib celery
3   cups chopped red potatoes
6   cups shredded romaine
2   cups cherry tomato halves
·   Bleu Cheese Buttermilk Dressing

Combine the olive oil, hot sauce and paprika in a large dish. Add the chicken and toss to coat. Marinate, covered, in the refrigerator for 30 to 60 minutes. Cut the carrot and celery lengthwise into 12 thin strips each using a vegetable peeler. Place in a bowl of ice water. Let stand for 30 minutes. Bring the potatoes and water to cover to a boil in a saucepan. Cook for 15 minutes or until tender. Drain and let stand until cool. Drain the chicken, discarding the marinade. Place on a grill rack coated with nonstick cooking spray. Grill for 5 minutes on each side or until the chicken is cooked through. Cut diagonally cross grain into thin slices. Arrange the romaine on 6 individual serving plates. Arrange the potatoes, carrot strips, celery strips, chicken and tomato halves on each serving of romaine. Drizzle with the Bleu Cheese Buttermilk Dressing. Yield: 6 servings.

Bleu Cheese Buttermilk Dressing

1/2   cup low-fat buttermilk
1/2   cup fat-free plain yogurt
3   tablespoons white wine vinegar
1   teaspoon sugar
1/2   teaspoon salt
1/2   teaspoon coarsely ground pepper
1/2   cup thinly sliced green onions
1/2   cup (2 ounces) crumbled bleu cheese

Combine the buttermilk, yogurt, wine vinegar, sugar, salt and pepper in a bowl and whisk until blended. Stir in the green onions and cheese.

Restaurant:
Crook's By the River

Chef:
Horacio Mendoza

Owner:
Susan A. Martin

SESAME PRAWNS WITH CRISPY GINGER

Restaurant:
Deluxe

Chef:
Aaron Peterson

Owner:
John Malejan

2/3	cup soy sauce
1/3	cup rice wine vinegar
1/3	cup fresh orange juice
1/4	cup sesame seeds
2	tablespoons chopped fresh ginger
2	tablespoons chopped fresh cilantro
2	cups canola oil
1	cup thinly sliced peeled ginger
2	tablespoons canola oil
1	red bell pepper, chopped
1	green bell pepper, chopped
1	red onion, chopped
32	large fresh shrimp, peeled, deveined
1	cup chopped green onions
2	tablespoons chopped garlic
1	pound vermicelli, cooked, drained, chilled

Combine the soy sauce, wine vinegar, orange juice, sesame seeds, chopped ginger and cilantro in a bowl and mix well. Let stand for 1 hour. Heat 2 cups canola oil in a skillet to 375 degrees. Add the thinly sliced ginger. Fry until golden brown and crispy. Remove to paper towels to drain. Heat 2 tablespoons canola oil in a wok over high heat. Add the red pepper, green pepper, red onion and shrimp. Stir-fry until the shrimp are nearly pink. Add the soy sauce mixture, green onions and garlic and mix well. Add the pasta and toss to mix well. Place the pasta in 4 individual serving bowls, placing 8 shrimp in each and drizzling with the sauce. Top each portion with the crisp-fried ginger. Serve immediately. Yield: 4 servings.

CAROLINA CHOWDER

1½	cups finely chopped onions
¾	cup finely chopped celery
1	cup butter
1½	cups flour
1	(32-ounce) can clam juice, heated
8	cups milk, scalded
1	cup dry cocktail sherry
2	teaspoons thyme
1½	teaspoons Tabasco sauce
·	Salt and pepper to taste
24	cherrystone clams, steamed, chopped
1	pound small shrimp, peeled, deveined
1	(8-ounce) can crab meat
1	pound bay scallops (optional)
8	to 10 small red potatoes, chopped, steamed

Sauté the onions and celery in the butter in a skillet until translucent. Stir in the flour. Cook for 3 to 5 minutes or until the mixture has the appearance of wet sand, stirring constantly and adding additional butter if needed. Remove from the heat. Add the clam juice, milk and cocktail sherry 1 at a time, whisking constantly until smooth. Return to the heat. Bring to a boil, whisking constantly. Add the thyme, Tabasco sauce, salt and pepper. Reduce the heat. Simmer until the flour has cooked out of the chowder, skimming the top several times. Add the clams, shrimp, crab meat and bay scallops. Cook until tender. Stir in the potatoes and adjust the seasonings. May add additional milk or hot clam juice if the chowder is too thick. Yield: 1 gallon.

Note: Do not substitute cooking sherry for the dry sherry. May use a combination of hot clam juice and chicken stock. May substitute half-and-half for ⅓ of the milk.

Restaurant:
Elijah's Restaurant

Chefs:
Vincent Drayton and
Kathy Seagraves

Owner:
River Enterprises, Inc.

Restaurant:
Figure Eight Island Yacht Club

Executive Chef:
Christian T. Clements
(recipe contributor)

Sous Chef:
Stephen Custer

GARLIC PESTO ROASTED RED SNAPPER WITH CEDAR SMOKED PIMENTO CHEESE

3	tablespoons fresh basil
1	clove of elephant garlic
2	tablespoons grated pecorino cheese
2	tablespoons roasted pine nuts
1	cup unfiltered virgin olive oil
1	(4-pound) red snapper, filleted
2	green lettuce leaves
·	Cedar Smoked Pimento Cheese

Process the basil, garlic, cheese, pine nuts and olive oil in a blender until smooth. Place the fish in a lightly oiled sauteuse pan. Spread generously with the pesto. Cover with the lettuce leaves to keep the fish moist. Bake at 350 degrees for 15 minutes or until the fish flakes easily. Discard the lettuce. Place Cedar Smoked Pimento Cheese on serving plates. Arrange the fish fillets on top. Yield: 4 servings.

CEDAR SMOKED PIMENTO CHEESE

2	cups grated sharp Cheddar cheese
½	cup finely chopped, seeded peeled pimentos
½	cup mayonnaise
1	tablespoon salt
·	Freshly ground pepper to taste

Place an untreated 2x2-inch piece of red cedar in a large saucepan. Light the wood with a torch. Let the wood burn until it looks fully burnt. Place the lid on the saucepan to extinguish the flame. Combine the cheese, pimentos, mayonnaise, salt and pepper in a small heatproof bowl and mix well. Place in the saucepan and cover with the lid. Let stand for 30 minutes. Remove the bowl from the saucepan and mix well again.

Tammy's Fish House Pasta Salad

1	(16-ounce) package bow tie pasta
1	cup mayonnaise
1/4	cup red wine vinegar
1/4	cup chopped fresh parsley
2	tablespoons chopped fresh oregano
•	Minced garlic to taste
•	Salt and pepper to taste
•	Sugar to taste
1	cup broccoli florets
1	cup chopped onion
1	cup cauliflowerets
1/2	cup chopped red bell pepper
1/2	cup chopped green bell pepper
1 1/2	pounds cooked shrimp

Cook the pasta using the package directions and drain. Combine the mayonnaise, red wine vinegar, parsley, oregano, garlic, salt, pepper and sugar in a bowl and mix well. Combine the pasta, broccoli, onion, cauliflowerets, red pepper and green pepper in a large bowl and toss to mix well. Add the mayonnaise mixture and mix well. Add the shrimp and toss to mix well. Chill in the refrigerator until serving time. Serve on lettuce-lined serving plates. Yield: 6 to 8 servings.

Restaurant:
Fish House Grill

Chef:
Tammy Shaw

Owners:
Johnnie and Estelle Baker

CRAB MEAT-STUFFED PORTABELLO MUSHROOM AND PASTA WITH GOAT CHEESE CREAM SAUCE

Restaurant:
Gardenias

Sous Chef:
Kathy Bahn

Owner:
Colin Eagles

1	large portabello
4	ounces backfin crab meat, drained, flaked
1	tablespoon olive oil
1	tablespoon minced chives
·	Salt and pepper to taste
1	tablespoon olive oil
1	tablespoon minced shallot
1	teaspoon minced garlic
¼	cup marsala
½	cup veal stock
½	cup whipping cream
1½	ounces goat cheese
4	ounces pasta, cooked, drained
¼	cup julienned red plum tomato
¼	cup julienned yellow tomato
½	cup torn mâche, arugula or spinach

Brush the mushroom with a small amount of olive oil. Place on a grill rack. Grill for 1 minute on each side. Combine the crab meat, 1 tablespoon olive oil, chives, salt and pepper in a bowl and mix well. Pack on top of the grilled mushroom. Place in a baking pan. Bake at 350 degrees for 10 minutes. Heat 1 tablespoon olive oil in a medium sauté pan over medium-high heat. Add the shallot and garlic. Cook until light brown. Remove from the heat. Add the marsala and veal stock. Cook over high heat until the liquid is reduced by half. Add the whipping cream and goat cheese. Cook until almost reduced by half. Add the pasta and salt and pepper to taste and toss to mix well. Add the tomatoes and mâche and mix well. Place in the center of a serving plate. Top with the crab-stuffed mushroom. Yield: 1 serving.

FRIED SOFT SHELL CRAB WITH TABASCO TARTAR AND CILANTRO POTATO SALAD

- 2 cups milk
- 1 egg
- · Flour
- · Salt and pepper to taste
- 4 soft shell crabs, cleaned
- · Vegetable oil for frying
- · Cilantro Potato Salad
- · Tabasco Tartar
- · Sprigs of fresh cilantro

Beat the milk and egg in a bowl. Season the flour with salt and pepper. Dip the crabs in the egg mixture and then dredge in the flour mixture. Fry the crabs in 360-degree vegetable oil in a 10-inch skillet for 4 to 5 minutes or until golden brown. Drain on paper towels. Spoon Cilantro Potato Salad onto each serving plate. Place a fried crab on each mound and top with Tabasco Tartar. Garnish with fresh cilantro. Yield: 4 servings.

Note: Ask your local fishmonger to properly clean the crabs.

CILANTRO POTATO SALAD

- 4 cups fingerling or new potato halves
- 1 cup chopped celery
- ½ cup mayonnaise
- ¼ cup Dijon mustard
- ¾ cup chopped fresh cilantro
- · Salt and pepper to taste

Steam the potatoes in a steamer until tender. Let stand until cool. Combine the potatoes, celery, mayonnaise, Dijon mustard, cilantro and salt and pepper to taste in a bowl and mix well. Chill, covered, in the refrigerator.

TABASCO TARTAR

- 1 cup mayonnaise
- 3 tablespoons sweet pickle relish
- · Juice of 1 lemon
- 1 tablespoon Worcestershire sauce
- · Tabasco sauce to taste
- 2 green onions, minced
- 1 tablespoon Creole seasoning or blackening seasoning

Combine the mayonnaise, pickle relish, lemon juice, Worcestershire sauce, Tabasco sauce, green onions and Creole seasoning in a bowl and mix well. Chill, covered, in the refrigerator.

Restaurant:
Harvest Moon Food and Spirits

Chef:
James Bain

Owner:
James Bain

GROUPER EXTRAVAGANZA

Restaurant:
Jerry's Food, Wine, and Spirits

Chef:
Brent Williams

Owner:
Jerry Rouse

¼	cup butter
3	tablespoons olive oil or extra-virgin olive oil
4	(6- to 8-ounce) skinned grouper fillets
·	Salt and pepper to taste
·	Flour
1	cup chardonnay
2	tablespoons julienned yellow onion
2	tablespoons chopped green onions
2	tablespoons chopped celery with leaves
1	tablespoon capers
1	cup whipping cream
·	Juice of 2 lemons
1	cup cooked deluxe crab meat
16	large shrimp, cooked, peeled, deveined
·	Chopped fresh parsley to taste (optional)
4	(⅛-inch-thick) lemon slices

Heat the butter and olive oil in a skillet over medium heat until the butter melts. Season the fish with salt and pepper. Sprinkle lightly with flour. Add to the hot skillet. Fry until golden brown and the fish flakes easily. Remove to paper towels to drain. Drain the skillet and return to the heat. Add the wine, stirring to deglaze the skillet. Add the onion, green onions, celery and undrained capers. Cook for 1 minute, adding additional butter if necessary. Stir in the whipping cream and lemon juice. Return the fried fish to the skillet. Add the crab meat and shrimp. Cook until the shrimp turn pink; do not overcook. Adjust the seasonings. Sprinkle with parsley. Place 1 fish fillet and 4 shrimp on each serving plate. Spoon the sauce over the seafood. Arrange a slice of lemon on top. Yield: 4 servings.

NEW MEXICAN GREEN CHILE STEW

8	slices bacon, chopped
2	ribs celery, finely chopped
2	carrots, finely chopped
2	large yellow onions, chopped
1	red onion, chopped
2½	pounds boneless pork shoulder, trimmed, cooked, cut into 1-inch cubes
15	Anaheim chiles, roasted, peeled, seeded, chopped
5	poblano chiles, roasted, peeled, seeded, chopped
5	serrano chiles, minced
2	(26-ounce) cans mild green chiles
2	cups chopped cilantro
1	pound Roma tomatoes, chopped
8	cloves of garlic, roasted, minced
1	pound red potatoes, cut into bite-size pieces
1	teaspoon cumin
1	tablespoon Mexican oregano
1	tablespoon coarse salt
1	teaspoon coarsely ground black pepper
3	quarts water
2	tablespoons corn oil

Fry the bacon in a stockpot until crisp. Add the celery, carrots and onions. Cook until the onions are translucent. Add the cooked pork, chiles, cilantro, tomatoes, garlic and potatoes. Stir in the cumin, oregano, salt, pepper, water and corn oil. Bring to a boil and reduce the heat. Simmer for 1½ hours. Adjust the seasonings. Yield: 12 servings.

Restaurant:
K-38 Baja Grill

Owner:
Josh Vach

Restaurant:
Porters Neck Country Club

Executive Chef:
Mike Stanley

Sous Chef:
Beth Flaherty
(recipes contributor)

NUTTED WILD RICE SALAD

1	cup wild rice
5½	cups stock or water
1	cup pecans
1	cup golden raisins
·	Zest of 1 orange
¼	cup chopped mint
4	scallions, chopped
¼	cup olive oil
⅓	cup orange juice
1½	teaspoons salt
·	Pepper to taste

Combine the rice and stock in a saucepan. Cook, covered, for 45 minutes. Chill in the refrigerator. Add the pecans, raisins, orange zest, mint, scallions, olive oil, orange juice, salt and pepper and mix well. Serve at room temperature or chilled. May add other dried fruits such as dried cranberries. Yield: 6 servings.

CHOCOLATE BOURBON PECAN PIE

3	tablespoons butter
2	ounces semisweet chocolate
3	eggs
1	cup light corn syrup
½	cup sugar
1½	teaspoons vanilla extract
¼	teaspoon salt
2	tablespoons bourbon
1½	cups chopped pecans
1	cup miniature chocolate chips
1	partially baked (9-inch) pie shell

Melt the butter and 2 ounces chocolate in a saucepan. Combine the eggs, corn syrup, sugar, vanilla and salt in a bowl and mix well. Stir in the bourbon, pecans and ¾ cup of the chocolate chips. Add the melted chocolate mixture and mix well. Pour into the partially baked pie shell. Sprinkle with the remaining ¼ cup chocolate chips. Bake at 350 degrees for 40 minutes or until puffed and set. Yield: 8 servings.

MOUSSAKA

2	medium eggplant	2	cloves of garlic, minced
	Salt to taste	1	teaspoon salt
1	medium onion, finely chopped	¼	teaspoon ground cinnamon
1	cup olive oil	⅛	teaspoon ground allspice
2	pounds lean ground beef or lamb, or 1 pound of each	⅛	teaspoon pepper
		¾	cup dry bread crumbs
½	cup chardonnay	¾	cup flour
2	medium tomatoes, peeled, seeded, diced	1	cup grated Romano or Parmesan cheese
¼	cup tomato purée	•	Yogurt Sauce
3	tablespoons chopped Italian parsley		

Restaurant:
The Surf Club

Chef:
Craig LaBreche

Peel the eggplant and slice ½ inch thick. Sprinkle with salt. Place on a rack in a pan. Let stand for 30 minutes. Sauté the onion in 2 tablespoons of the olive oil in a large skillet over medium heat for 5 minutes or until soft. Add the ground beef. Cook for 8 to 12 minutes, stirring until the ground beef is brown and crumbly; drain. Add the wine, tomatoes, tomato purée, parsley, garlic, 1 teaspoon salt, cinnamon, allspice and pepper. Cook until most of the liquid has evaporated, stirring frequently. Remove from the heat and stir in the bread crumbs. Pat the eggplant dry with a clean towel. Dust each slice with the flour. Fry the eggplant in the remaining olive oil in a large skillet over medium heat for 1 to 2 minutes on each side or until light brown. Arrange ½ of the eggplant in a greased baking dish. Layer ⅓ of the cheese, the ground beef mixture, ½ of the remaining cheese and the remaining eggplant in the prepared dish. Pour the Yogurt Sauce over the layers and sprinkle with the remaining cheese. Bake at 375 degrees for 40 to 45 minutes or until golden brown. Let stand for 10 to 15 minutes before serving.
Yield: 8 to 10 servings.

YOGURT SAUCE

4	eggs	¼	cup sour cream
1½	tablespoons flour	⅛	teaspoon nutmeg
2	cups plain yogurt	•	Salt and pepper to taste

Whisk the eggs in a 2-quart saucepan. Add the flour, yogurt, sour cream, nutmeg and salt and pepper. Cook over medium heat for 6 to 8 minutes or until thickened, stirring constantly.

Restaurant:
Sweet and Savory Bake Shop

Chef:
Dave Herring

Owner:
Dave Herring

ITALIAN BREAD

1	cup semolina flour
1	tablespoon salt
1/2	tablespoon sugar
2	tablespoons dry yeast
2	cups water, at room temperature
5¼	cups high gluten flour

Mix 1 cup semolina flour, salt, sugar and yeast in a bowl. Add the water. Stir for 1 minute or until smooth. Stir in the 5¼ cups flour. Knead on a floured surface for 15 minutes or until smooth and elastic. Cover with a damp cloth. Let rise for 30 minutes or until doubled in bulk. Punch the dough down. Divide the dough into 2 equal portions. Shape each portion into a round loaf. Place each loaf on a baking sheet sprinkled with cornmeal. Let rise for 10 minutes. Spray the loaves with water. Bake at 450 degrees for 30 minutes or until the loaves test done, spraying with water every 10 minutes. Yield: 2 round loaves.

FLOURLESS CHOCOLATE TORTE

2	cups butter
4	cups semisweet chocolate chips
12	eggs, at room temperature
2	tablespoons vanilla extract
1	tablespoon rum

Bring the butter to a boil in a saucepan. Add to the chocolate chips in a bowl and stir until smooth. Place the bowl over hot water if needed to completely melt the chocolate chips, stirring constantly. Whip the eggs in a mixer bowl for 5 to 10 minutes or until of full volume. Add the vanilla and rum and mix well. Fold in the melted chocolate mixture. Pour into 2 nonstick 8-inch cake pans. Bake at 375 degrees for 15 to 20 minutes or until the top is just set. The cakes will still feel loose. Chill for 8 hours. Yield: 24 to 32 servings.

LINGUINI WITH CLAM SAUCE

1½	teaspoons	flour
1	teaspoon	black pepper
½	teaspoon	red pepper flakes
6	tablespoons	olive oil
2	tablespoons	basil garlic pesto
¼	cup	white wine
1	cup	clam juice
1	tablespoon	grated Romano cheese
32	ounces	linguini, cooked
1⅓	cups	chopped clams

Mix the flour, black pepper and red pepper flakes together. Heat the olive oil in a large skillet over medium-high heat. Stir in the flour mixture and pesto. Add the wine and clam juice. Bring to a boil and reduce the heat. Add the cheese. Simmer until thickened, stirring constantly. Add the linguini and clams and toss to mix well. Serve immediately. Yield: 4 servings.

Restaurant:
Vinnie's Steak House and Tavern

Recipe Contributor:
Charles Anderson

Chef:
Scott Spencer

Owners:
Brenda Chandler, Thad Faulk,
and C. L. Carmichael

We gratefully acknowledge the financial assistance of the following corporations
and individual friends of the Junior League of Wilmington, as it exemplifies their support
for the purpose of the Junior League of Wilmington and their concern for
the children and families of our community.

GRAND PATRON

Bradley - Barnes Construction Company, Inc.

PATRONS

Dover Mortgage Company
Eugenia Goff
Bobby Moore
Clint and Amy North

Stork's Nest
Sutton Council Furniture
Teacher's Aid
Jacqueline Warwick

SPONSORS

Bill and Rosalie Avery
Beth and Bob Cherry
Angie and Bill Cline
Bonnie R. Culbreth
Dr. and Mrs. Douglas F. De Groote
Four Seasons Cleaners
Mr. and Mrs. Douglas P. Fritz
Valeri Froneberger
Furniture Choices
Hilda Godwin's
Mrs. David B. Grinnell
Janet Poole Hicks
Fran La Fontaine

Paula Lentz
Mrs. William O. McMillan, Jr.
Sylvia Miller
Ann and Patrick Moore
Dr. and Mrs. Charles Nance
Jane and Fred Rippy III
Doris Humphrey Ruffner
Carol C. Schenck
Emily Sloan
Mr. and Mrs. John W. Smith
Paula Sneeden
Joe and Kenda Walter
Mr. and Mrs. William Donald Wright

RECIPE TESTERS

Seaboard to Sideboard is a collection of 236 recipes selected from over 600 recipes submitted. We thank all of those who shared their recipes and especially those who tested them.

Annie Anthony
Beth Banick
Glenda Bradley
Melva Calder
Sharon Chadwick
Christine Chappell
Angie Cline
Gretchen Estes
Angela Gilbert
Scott Gilbert
Missy Goetz
Jackie Gooch

Beth Harry
Jane Hawthorne
Lee Hawthorne
Mary High
Michelle Hildreth
Margaret Lamm
Mary Beth Laurie
Valerie Lazzari
Betsy Lewis
Mary Loughren
Stephanie Mannen
Katherine Marapese

Shannon Maus
Barbara McInnes
Ann Moore
Krista Combs Ray
Elizabeth Redenbaugh
Ann Robertson
Becky Shannon
Sarah S. Stanley
Angela Turner
Kim Whitfield
Porter Young

CONTRIBUTORS

We would like to thank the following people for contributing their recipes or other support.

Sue Ellen Abrams
Anne van Amerongen
Terry C. Andrews
Annie M. Anthony
Kelly B. Armstrong
Bill Atwill, Ph.D.
Kathy McGrew Babb
Estelle Baker
Ede D. Baldridge
Toni Thompson Barfield
Catherine Barrett-Fischer
MaryPaul Beall
Nancy Beeler
Bridget Bender
Shannon Benedict
Darlene Bennett
Patricia Donovan Bennett
Carey Beyle
Kathryn W. Black
Anne McGhee Bogen
Marsha Bonner
Barbie Bowers
Farah Boyce
Charlene Boyd
Buddy Bradley
Glenda H. Bradley
Scott Bradley
Nancy Tinga Braswell
Anna Bray
Barbara M. Brennaman
Cissie Bridger
Karen McAden Broadway
Joan Brooks
Stephanie Brooks
Judy B. Brown
Linda Brown
Tracy Brown
Holly Horton Bullard

Zina Burney
Susan Deibert Butler
Deborah Lewis Capra
Nancy Carter
Winnie Carter
Beth Chadwick
Sharon Chadwick
Barbara F. Chatham
Katharine Nixon Cheek
Beth Chadwick Cherry
Angie Chatham Cline
Jane Cline
Virginia Colantuono
Teresa H. Coleman
Robert F. Coleman, Jr.
Bessie Cooke
Elizabeth Cooper
Sue Trask Coupland
Margaret Crouch
Cathy Reichardt Cypher
Bud Davis
Susan M. DeGroote
Sara F. Duncan
Nancy T. Efird
Karin Egan
Jennifer C. Elam
Mauarine Ashton Elebash
Gretchen Estes
Donna Evans
Catherine McGregor Faver
Barry Fischer
Julie E. Fisher
Kristin Freccia
Beth Frederick
Cheryl Fulp
Lois Furr
Fairye M. Gilster
Alice Tennille Givens

Hilda Sellars Godwin
Missy Goetz
Walker Golder
Mary Frere Murchison Gornto
Bonnie Grady
Margaret Alexius Greene
Lou M. Greer
Verna H. Hallman
Patricia H. Ham
Susan Hance
Liz Moore Hansen
Marshall Taylor Harper
Leba Harrington
Jane Harshbarger
Care Heeks
Betsy Rhodes Herring
Dave and Kimber Herring
Erin Hester
Janet Poole Hicks
Mary High
Michelle Hildreth
Virginia Ashburn Hill
Michelle Hoban
Barbara B. Hoenig
Gina Q. Holdford
Marie Horn
Claude Howell
Elizabeth Hunter
Barbara Bear Jamison
Bob Jenkins
Amy T. Johnson
Sue Edwards Jones
Sara Jordan
Carol Stuhr Kays
Alicia C. Keith
Emeline Keith
Dianne R. Kelly
Jil Kerekes

Lisa F. King
Robyn Brickner Krassas
Fran Hosley LaFontaine
Margaret Lamm
Paula T. Lanier
Mary Beth Laurie
Valerie Lazzari
Isabel Lehto
Amy K. Lennon
Paula Lentz
Lucy Lester
Zonya Letson
Betsy Wilkinson Lewis
Mary Ellen Loughren
Louise Williams Love
Stephanie Mannen
Shannon Mansfield
Katherine Thomas Marapese
Mary Louise Marks
Meg Massey
Amy Maultsby
Shannon Maus
Ashley Greer McAlpin
Ann McCall-Moore
Jerry McEntire
Kay McEntire
Barbara McInnes
Kathy McKenzie
Karen McManus
Frances McMillan
Cyndi McNeill
Carolyn Medley
Nancy Mihle
Nancy G. Miller
Plutina Morrow
Arlene Nail
Linda Patton Nance
Suzanne Smith Nash

Bill Neal
Tannis F. Nelson
Jenny Newell
Shirley Nolan
David Nye
Jan Oden
Patti Pardee
Connie Newman Parker
Bette Parrett
Karla Patrick
Virginia Pierce
Mary-Emily J. Pitt
Susan Pleasants
Shari Porter
Melanie M. Powers
Sharon Rambeaut
Donna Ray
Krista Combs Ray
Elizabeth S. Redenbaugh
Mary-Louise Rhodes
Carrie Roberts
Mrs. James H. Robinson
Julie Robinson
Robin Wicks Robinson
Maryann Oakley Robison
Jane Gregg Rogers
Patricia Morris Roseman
Anne Russell, Ph.D.
Polly Rust
Mary Beth Sanders
Becky Shannon
Malinda Sharp
Mickie Sharpe
Fred Shaw
Joe Shepard
Kathleen Sherman
Wendy Wright Simmons
Louise Sloan

Ange Smith
Harriet H. Smith
Tavia H. Smith
Paula Sneeden
Ronald Sparks
Albert Stevens
Nancy Stevens
John Stokes, M.D.
Barbara White Stutts
Elizabeth Norfleet Sugg
Amy Lynn Sutton
Beverly Tetterton
Karen G. Thompson
Gail Tice
Elsie Orrell Tilson
Beth Trice
Ed Turberg
Angela Babb Turner
Melodye Visser, M.D.
Claudia Vurnakes
Greg Watkins
Peggy Weymouth
Lucy Wheeless
Marcia Wiggins
Gibbs Holmes Willard
Meg Williamson
Beverly Wilson
Missye Wilson
Marie Wood
Martha Wortman
Jim Wright
Porter E. Young
Connie Stewart Yow

INDEX

BIBLIOGRAPHY

Bache, Ellyn, ed. *Wilmington and Its Beaches*. Wilmington, N.C.: Banks Channel Books, 1993.

Bivins, John Jr., and St. John's Museum of Art, Historic Wilmington Foundation. *Wilmington Furniture 1720–1860*. Wilmington, N.C., 1989.

Bloodworth, Mattie. *History of Pender County, North Carolina*. Richmond, Va.: Dietz Printing Co., 1947.

Boykin, Edward Carrington. *Sea Devil of the Confederacy: The Story of the* Florida *and Her Captain, John Newland Maffitt*. New York: Funk & Wagnalls, 1959.

Cashman, Diane Cobb. *Cape Fear Adventure: An Illustrated History of Wilmington*. 2d ed. Woodland Hills, Calif.: Windsor Publications, 1982.

Catton, Bruce. *The American Heritage Picture of the Civil War, The Epic Struggle of the Blue and the Gray*. 1992. Bonanza Books. Originally published: New York: American Heritage Pub. Co., 1960.

Dobson, Helen E. *Our Living Strength: a Historical Sketch of First Baptist Church, Wilmington, N.C.* Wilmington, N.C.: Wilmington Print Co., 1958.

Hall, Lewis Philip. *Land of the Golden River*. Vol. 1, Old Times on the Seacoast. Wilmington, N.C.: Hall, 1975–1980.

Johnson, George, Jr. *Rose O'Neale Greenhow and the Blockade Runners*. Printed in Canada, 1995.

Lefler, Hugh Talmage, ed. *North Carolina History Told By Contemporaries*. 3d ed., rev. and enl. Chapel Hill: The University of North Carolina Press, 1956.

Lefler, Hugh T., and William S. Powell. *Colonial North Carolina: A History. A History of the American Colonies in Thirteen Volumes*. New York: Charles Scribner's Sons, 1973.

Lennon, Donald R., and Ida Brooks Kellam, eds. *The Wilmington Town Book: 1743–1778*. Raleigh, N.C.: Division of Archives and History, North Carolina.

Moore, Louis T. *Stories Old and New of the Cape Fear Region as told by Louis T. Moore*. Memorial ed. Wilmington, N.C.: Wilmington Printing Company, 1956.

Old Wilmington Guidebook. The Junior League of Wilmington, North Carolina, Inc., 1978, 105.

Powell, William S., ed. *Dictionary of North Carolina Biography*. 6 vols. Chapel Hill: University of North Carolina Press, 1979.

Powell, William Stevens. *North Carolina Through Four Centuries*. Chapel Hill, N.C.: University of North Carolina Press, 1989.

Preik, Brooks Newton. *Haunted Wilmington and the Cape Fear Coast*. Wilmington, N.C.: Banks Channel Books, 1995.

Rankin, Hugh F. *The Pirates of Colonial North Carolina*. Raleigh: Division of Archives and History, 1983.

Russell, Anne, Ph.D. *Wilmington: A Pictorial History*. Norfolk, Va.: The Donning Company, 1981.

Scott, Blackie. *It's Fun to Entertain, A Humorous Factual Creative Guide to Entertaining*. Atlanta, Ga.: Peachtree Publishers, Ltd., 1983.

Seapker, Janet K., ed. *Time, Talent, Tradition: Five Essays on The Cultural History of the Lower Cape Fear Region, North Carolina*. Wilmington, N.C.: Cape Fear Museum, 1995.

Shingleton, Royce. *High Seas Confederate: The Life and Times of John Newland Maffitt*. Columbia, S.C.: University of South Carolina Press, 1994.

Spencer, Robin, ed. *Whistler, A Retrospective*. 1989, 1991 edition. New York: Distributed by Random House, N.Y.

Sprunt, James. *Chronicles of the Cape Fear River, 1660–1916*. 2d ed. Raleigh, N.C.: Edwards and Broughton Printing Co., 1916.

Stick, David. *Bald Head: A History of Smith Island and Cape Fear*. Wendell, N.C.: Broadfoot Pub., 1985.

Stick, David. *Graveyard of the Atlantic, Shipwrecks of the North Carolina Coast*. Chapel Hill, N.C.: The University of North Carolina Press, 1952.

The William Reaves Collection. Local History Room. New Hanover County Public Library.

Wilmington Antiques, reprinted from *The Magazine Antiques*, December 1980; Lower Cape Fear Historical Society, Wilmington, North Carolina.

Wilmington Journal, "Yellow Fever Plague," November 17, 1862.

Wilmington Morning Star, "Exhibition tests architectural IQ," December 16, 1987, 1D.

Wilmington Morning Star, "The Hidden Treasures of Sugarloaf," March 31, 1989, 1D.

Wilmington Morning Star, "Renowned Wilmington Artist Dies," February 5, 1997, 1A.

Wilmington Morning Star, "Guidebook Insert 'Azalea Gold,'" April 10, 1997.

Wilmington Star-News, "Members Only," September 19, 1993, 1D.

Wilmington Star-News, "Made by Black Hands," February 20, 1994, 1D.

Wilmington Star-News, "Tour by Candlelight," November 26, 1995, 1D.

Wilmington Star-News, "The Wilmington 10," February 18, 1996, 1D.

Wilmington Star-News, "Port City by Candlelight," December 1, 1996, 1D.

Wilmington Star-News, "The Wilmington Connection," February 9, 1997, 1D.

Wilmington Star-News, "Own a Piece of Claude Howell's Personal Collection," September 21, 1997, 1D.

Wrenn, Tony P., with photographs by William Edmund Barrett. *Wilmington, North Carolina, An Architectural and Historical Portrait*. Wilmington, N.C.: The Junior League of Wilmington, North Carolina, Inc., 1984.

References Cited

p. 20 Arthur Dobbs quote: *Southern Living Magazine* (June 1997), page 30.

p. 20 Charles Darwin quote: *Old Wilmington Guidebook*, by the Junior League of Wilmington, North Carolina, Inc. (1978), page 105.

p. 49 Alfred Moore quote: *Literature of the Lower Cape Fear*, by Stephen Cymbalsky, page 42; *Time, Talent, Tradition: Five Essays on the Cultural History of the Lower Cape Fear Region*, edited by Janet K. Seapker (Cape Fear Museum, Wilmington, North Carolina, 1995).

p. 67 Quote from *Southern Living Magazine* (January 1991).

p. 77 *Guide to North Carolina Highway Historical Markers*, 8th edition, edited by Michael Hill (Division of Archives and History, Department of Cultural Resources, Raleigh, North Carolina, 1990), page 32.

p. 114 David Bryant Fulton [Jack Thorne, pseud.] quote: "Tender Recollections of Wilmington, N.C." In *Wilmington: A Pictorial History* by Anne Russell. Norfolk, Va.: The Donning Company/ Publishers, 1981.

p. 132 Robert Ruark quote: "The Old Man and The Boy." In *Carolina Yacht Club Chronicles* by Anne Russell. Wrightsville Beach, N.C.: Carolina Yacht Club, 1993.

Seaboard to Sideboard

Publications Committee • Junior League of Wilmington, North Carolina, Inc.
3803 Wrightsville Avenue • Downey Branch Office Park, Unit 9
Wilmington, North Carolina 28403 • (910) 799-7405

Please send me _____ copies of *Seaboard to Sideboard* @ $19.95 each $_____
Shipping @ $ 3.00 each $_____
Sales Tax (N.C. Residents Only) @ $ 1.20 each $_____
TOTAL $_____

Name _____

Address _____

City _____ State _____ Zip Code _____

Daytime Phone ( ) _____

Method of Payment

___ VISA ___ MasterCard ___ Check or Money Order payable to Junior League of Wilmington, N.C., Inc.

Account Number _____ Expiration Date _____

Signature _____

Seaboard to Sideboard

Publications Committee • Junior League of Wilmington, North Carolina, Inc.
3803 Wrightsville Avenue • Downey Branch Office Park, Unit 9
Wilmington, North Carolina 28403 • (910) 799-7405

Please send me _____ copies of *Seaboard to Sideboard* @ $19.95 each $_____
Shipping @ $ 3.00 each $_____
Sales Tax (N.C. Residents Only) @ $ 1.20 each $_____
TOTAL $_____

Name _____

Address _____

City _____ State _____ Zip Code _____

Daytime Phone ( ) _____

Method of Payment

___ VISA ___ MasterCard ___ Check or Money Order payable to Junior League of Wilmington, N.C., Inc.

Account Number _____ Expiration Date _____

Signature _____